1000 FLAGS BANNERS AND ENSIGNS

A Firefly Book

Published by Firefly Books Ltd. 2020
English edition © Firefly Books Ltd. 2020
All other rights © Olo Éditions, 2020
Text © Elisabeth Dumont-Le Cornec 2020
Flags © DR

First printing

Library of Congress Control Number: 2020939790

Library and Archives Canada Cataloguing in Publication
Title: 1000 flags : banners and ensigns / Elisabeth Dumont-Le Cornec.
Other titles: One thousand flags.
Names: Dumont-Le Cornec, Élisabeth, author.
Description: Translated from the French by Adriana Paradiso.
Identifiers: Canadiana 20200265962 | ISBN 9780228102588 (hardcover)
Subjects: LCSH: Flags—Pictorial works.
Classification: LCC CR101 .D85 2020 | DDC 929.9/2—dc23

Published in Canada by
Firefly Books Ltd.
50 Staples Avenue, Unit 1
Richmond Hill, Ontario
L4B 0A7

Published in the United States by
Firefly Books (U.S.) Inc.
P.O. Box 1338, Ellicott Station
Buffalo, New York
14205

Design: Philippe Marchand
Translation: Adriana Paradiso

Printed in Korea

FSC
MIX
Paper from
responsible sources
FSC® C140526

We acknowledge the financial support of the Government of Canada.

1000 FLAGS BANNERS AND ENSIGNS

Elisabeth Dumont-Le Cornec

FIREFLY BOOKS

Table of Contents

1

Anatomy of a Flag

2

The Toolbox

3

(Re)constructing the Past

4

A History of Nations

5

A Common Identity

6

The Flag as a Universal Medium

7

An Overview of Flags

CHAPTER 1

ANATOMY OF A FLAG

Both an emblem and a means of communication, a flag represents one's sense of belonging to a nation, culture, cause, history or camp. From a carved stick to the codified objects they are today, flags have significantly evolved since their inception. Nonetheless, a flag's strength lies in its simplicity and the effectiveness of its representation. Despite its limited toolbox, a flag embodies the body politic of a group or community.

MANY ORIGINS, ONE MEANING

Leaders have always used emblems to unite their troops, remain visible in battle, demonstrate their power and celebrate their victories.

The notion of flags began as carved staffs and painted signs. Around 2000 BCE, the Chinese attached banners made of woven silk to bamboo stalks. In ancient Rome, legions and cavalries used a standard, or "vexillum" (from the Latin), which were pieces of fringed fabric attached to a pole. That's why we refer to the study of flags as vexillolgy and someone who studies flags as a vexillologist. The origins of the English word "flag" are unknown, but the first known use of the word dates from the 16th century. The French word *drapeau* is borrowed from the Italian *drapello*, which was the "banner" of a feudal lord. Hung on a lance, it allowed soldiers to distinguish between their allies and enemies on the battlefield. In the 16th century, these banners became real flags and gained a new purpose, that of uniting a people, while remaining a way to identify and be identified in order to assert one's presence, to mark one's territory and to display one's strength. Some contemporary flags have retained the coat of arms tradition. Many tell a story from just one page of the country's recent history; others focus on the country's geography, values and political or religious views.

Vexillology is the study of flags, and a vexillogist is someone who studies flags.

The Parts of a Flag

A flag consists of several recurring physical elements that can be used to describe it.

A flagpole is a vertical staff, made of wood or metal, along which a flag is hoisted. The section of the flag closest to the pole is called the hoist. The fly is the section of the flag opposite the hoist, which "flaps" in the wind. The canton can refer to any quarter of the flag, but unless otherwise specified, it generally refers to the upper-left quarter, the side attached to the flagpole. It often stands out from the rest of the design on a flag, such as those of Greece, the United States of America, Malaysia and the Republic of China (a region commonly referred to as Taiwan).

The background color of the flag is called the field.

Double-sided

Most flags have the same design on both sides. One exception is Paraguay's flag, which is the only national flag to have a different design on each side.

FLAGPOLE
A wooden or metal vertical pole used to hoist the flag.

CANTON
This can be any quarter section of a flag, but generally refers to the upper-left quarter.

FLY
The part of the flag that flaps in the wind.

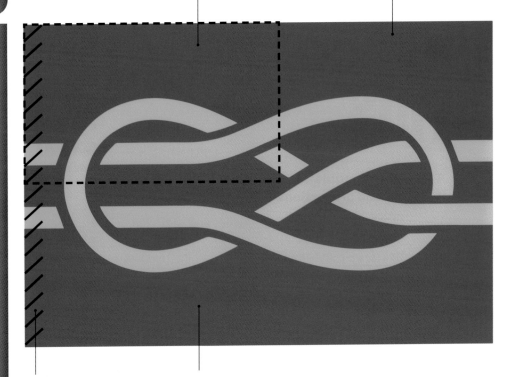

HOIST
The pole-side part of a flag, which does not flutter in the wind.

FIELD
The background color of a flag

FLAG OF THE INTERNATIONAL FEDERATION OF VEXILLOLOGICAL ASSOCIATIONS

A HISTORY OF RATIOS

A flag is distinguished by its colors but also by its shape and proportions.

The relationship between a flag's height and width determines its ratio (or proportions). A ratio of 2:3 means the flag's height measures 2 units and its width is 3 units (for example, 2 feet and 3 feet). The most common ratios are 1:2 and 2:3. For technical reasons, the proportions of flags are often adjusted in books, as in this book. Some flags come in a variety of shapes; for example, Belgium has an official version (13:15) and a civilian version (2:3), and Niger's flag is usually portrayed with a 6:7 ratio, but the official documentation regarding the adoption of its flag offers no standardization.

Only the flags of Switzerland and the Vatican are square (1:1). By contrast, Qatar's flag has a ratio of 11:28, giving it an elongated rectangular shape. Nepal's flag is unique in more ways than one: It is the smallest, it is taller than it is long (5:4 ratio) and it has cutouts. The two stacked triangles represent the Himalayas as well as the country's two religions: Buddhism and Hinduism. The blue border represents harmony and peace, and the crimson red, the national color, is symbolic of the bravery of the Nepalese people. Lastly, the sun and moon refer to both the royal families and leaders and to a prayer (a mantra) that asks for the nation to prosper as long as the astral bodies shine in the sky. Officially adopted in 1962, this flag is the combination of two flags.

Only the Nepalese flag is taller than it is wide, and it is also the only national flag that has cutouts.

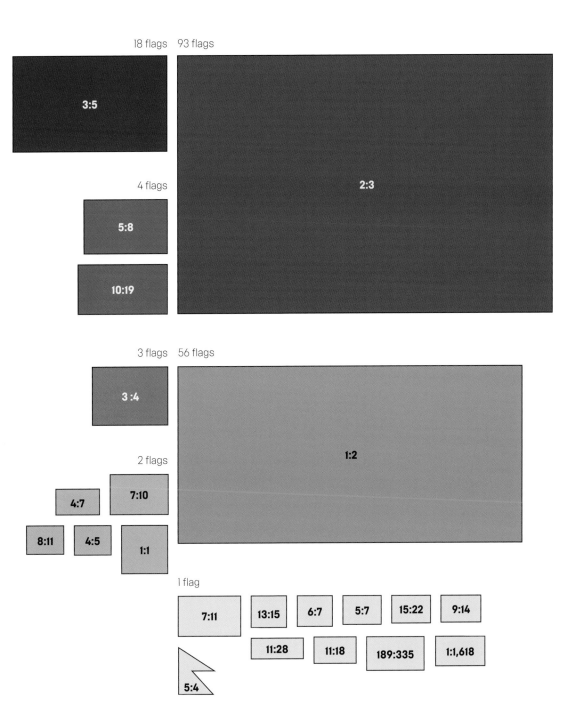

TYPES OF FLAGS

"Flag" is a broad term covering several different types of flags, which are mainly characterized by their usage.

A **flag** is a piece of fabric attached to a flagpole so that it can be displayed and fly in the wind, bearing the colors of a nation, province, organization, military unit or other group. A **standard** is mostly used as a rallying point in a battle or as an emblem. A **banner** was originally a feudal flag, a piece of fabric attached to a flagpole bearing the coat of arms or the symbol of the monarch. Banners were also often used in battle, much like standards. A **pennant** is a small, often triangular flag that is used for identification or signaling. In the military, pennants can be used by units who do not have a particular flag or standard. An **oriflamme** is a long and narrow ceremonial banner. An **ensign** is a flag flown on the main flagpole of a naval or merchant ship. It indicates the vessel's nationality, company or ownership, and ensigns can also be used to display a signal or provide information (such as a distress flag). Ensigns are often a variant of the national flag, but those used on military ships can differ greatly from the corresponding national flag. There are three types of ensigns: the one used on official ships (for example, customs and coast guard ships), the civil ensign flown by commercial or cruise ships, and the naval ensign of military ships. Some countries use the exact same flag for their national flag and ensign whereas others, like Japan, Germany and Luxembourg, have two. **Guidons** and **pennons** have primarily military (generally navy or cavalry) functions.

False Identity

Navigation "under a flag of convenience" refers to flying a national ensign that differs from the ship's actual ownership. In 2015, 71% of merchant vessels sailed under a flag of convenience. This is generally done to help lower the tax burden or to take advantage of laxer security and labor laws.

Figuratively Speaking

Flags are often symbolic of one's homeland, as in "honor the flag" or "defend the flag."

An exhibition of a large-scale
model of the Stars and Stripes
at the Smithsonian Institution
in 1914.

STRICT USAGE RULES

The displaying and handling of flags are subject to an established protocol at international and national levels, which are specific to each country.

All citizens must treat flags with respect. It is forbidden to fly a torn, dirty or discolored flag; to leave a flag wrapped around the flagpole; to let it touch the ground; to drag it in water; or to fly it at night, unless it is illuminated. For example, in France, Armenia, Egypt and Morocco, disrespecting the flag is punishable by imprisonment and/or fines. However, the Supreme Court of the United States and the European Court of Human Rights see those charges as an affront to freedom of expression. In the United States, those who burn the American flag during a protest are protected by the First Amendment.

An upside-down flag signifies that it has fallen into the hands of an enemy or signals distress. When a flag is being raised to the top of a flagpole, it is customary to salute the flag. At the end of the day, it is slowly brought down and folded according to standard practice. The Belgian flag is folded so that the black side remains on the outside, to help hide dirt. For the French flag, the blue side is on the outside in times of peace, but the red side is on the outer side in times of war. Adorning with flags is also a symbolic act. From country to country, public buildings (city halls, schools, hospitals, etc.) must fly the national flag, especially during official public ceremonies. During periods of mourning, the flag is flown at half-mast, meaning it is lowered halfway down the flagpole for a fixed period of time.

10,000 Yuan

That's how much (equivalent to about US$1,420) a French basketball player was fined for disrespecting the league's rules while playing for a Chinese team: He looked away from the Chinese flag during the national anthem.

No Special Treatment

When multiple flags fly together, they should all be the same size and arranged in alphabetical order.

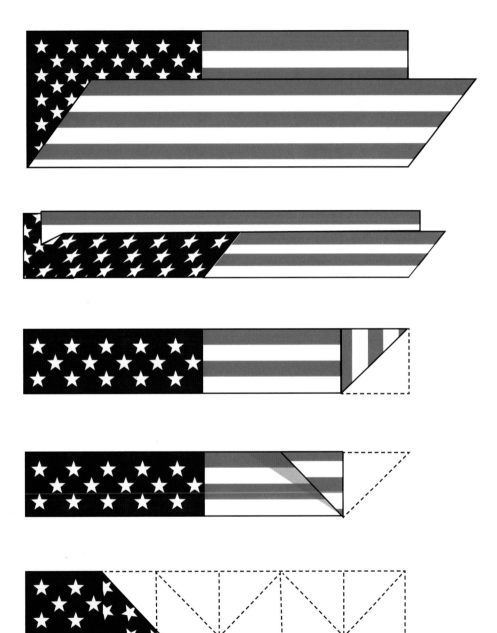

Teamwork

It takes two people to fold up the Australian flag like an accordion or to fold and roll up the British flag. Four people are required to fold the American flag into a triangle, and eight people are needed to fold the Canadian flag in eight. The folds are different for each country.

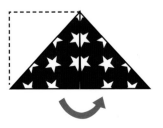

CHAPTER 2

THE TOOLBOX

See and be seen — that is the very essence of a flag. Shapes and colors are combined to that end. Each motif has a meaning, and the nations or groups use symbols to create their emblem. The same (or similar) elements are often used, but there are as many designs as there are nations. The variations are endless.

THE MOST COMMON COLORS

The most
common
colors are

1
red

2
blue

3
white

4
green

5
yellow

6
black

A flag is distinguished primarily by its colors. Hence we have expressions such as "sailing under false colors" and the British tradition of "Trooping the Colour."

"Trooping the Colour" is the name of the traditional parade that celebrates the birthday of the British sovereign. The term has been used since 1748.

While the first flags were monochromatic so they could more easily identify soldiers on the battlefield, the flags of today bear colors full of meaning. The most commonly used colors on national flags are red, blue, white, green, black and yellow. Next are orange and brown. Purple is not used, except for the parrot at the center of the flag of Dominica.

The color palette for flags is similar to that used in heraldry, but it has expanded since the end of the 20th century, with the emergence of pink and more than eight different shades of blue, from sky blue to dark indigo.

Most national flags are tricolored (78 out of 201), but they can contain up to 12 different colors or more — Mexico's flag has 15 colors! Then there are flags with four colors (51), two colors (38) and five colors (18). The combination of blue, white and red dominates European and North American flags, while red, white and green prevail in Asia. In Oceania, sea blue comes out ahead of red. In Africa, green and red vie for first place, edging out blue and yellow, which are almost equally represented.

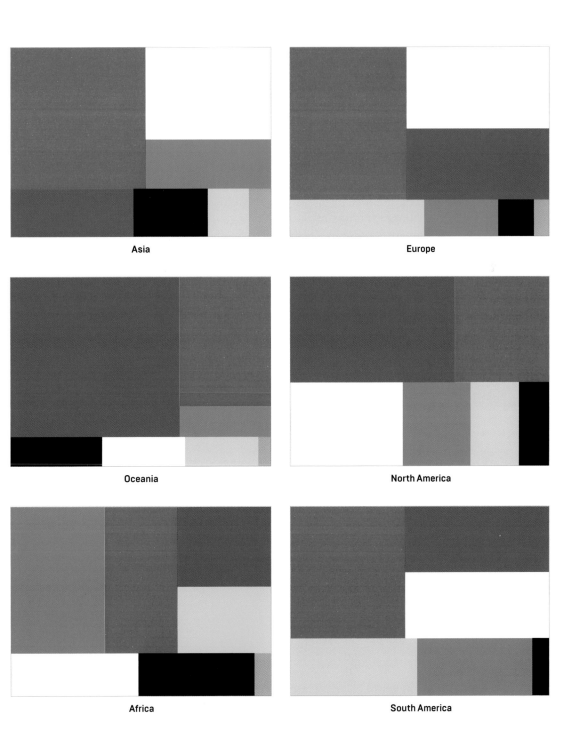

Asia

Europe

Oceania

North America

Africa

South America

White Is for Cease-Fire!

The custom of using a white flag to surrender existed in China as early as the Han Dynasty (206 BCE–220 CE), and was also used by Roman legionnaires in the first century. Its use gradually became widespread in Europe. In the 19th century, it was documented by conventions that tried to impose rules of conduct for times of war, which gave rise to international humanitarian laws. However, it was not until 1899, during the first Hague International Peace Conference, that its usage as a flag of truce was officially ratified, specified in Article 32 of the Convention with Respect to the Laws and Customs of War on Land: "An individual is considered as a parlementaire who is authorized by one of the belligerents to enter into communication with the other, and who carries a white flag. He has a right to inviolability, as well as the trumpeter, bugler, or drummer, the flag-bearer and the interpreter who may accompany him."

A white flag is now the sign of recognition and protection of every "parlementaire" responsible for negotiating peace. Its use imposes an end to hostilities and protects the person who waves it so that they may cross enemy lines and negotiate a truce, surrender or armistice. The carrier is bound by neutrality and must advance unarmed. Misuse of this emblem is strictly forbidden. White is often associated with peace (for example, the Pan-Slavic colors), but it can also be associated with purity (South Korea and Georgia). On the Lebanese flag, white refers to the snow on Mount Lebanon.

23

That's the number of countries that signed the Convention with Respect to the Laws and Customs of War on Land in The Hague on July 29, 1899. Today, 51 countries have ratified the Geneva Conventions, fundamental texts of international humanitarian law.

Like Snow

A white flag was for a long time a symbol of the Kingdom of France. The tricolor flag began to replace it between 1790 and 1815, before being definitively adopted in 1830.

Republic of Korea (South Korea)

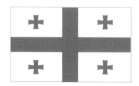

Georgia

Monaco

Lebanon

Anarchist flag (after 1968)

Black Is for Battle

Black is the color of mourning, and a black flag can evoke insurgency, danger, death, strength (Trinidad and Tobago) or the origin of a tribe (Papua New Guinea). Throughout history, a black flag has also been a symbol of anarchists, fascists and Islamist movements. In addition, it serves as the background of pirate flags. In France, black flags emerged during the July Revolution of 1830, when it began intermingling with the reg flag of the labor movement. It could be seen flying the following year in Lyon during the Canuts revolts and again during the Paris Commune in 1871, by which time the red flag had been outlawed. An anarchist newspaper founded in 1882 was titled *Le Drapeau noir* (the black flag). And it was a black flag that Louise Michel, a

> "No more red flags, dyed with the blood of our soldiers. I will wave the black flag to mourn our dead and our illusions."
>
> **Louise Michel**

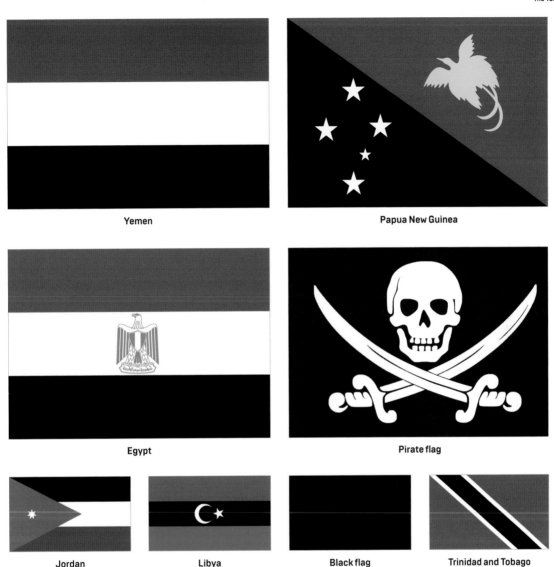

Yemen

Papua New Guinea

Egypt

Pirate flag

Jordan

Libya

Black flag

Trinidad and Tobago

prominent figure of libertarian anarchism, carried in Paris on March 9, 1883. She secured a black petticoat to a broomstick to protest with the unemployed. The black flag became the symbol of anarchists and the fight against injustice. At the start of the 20th century, anarchists around the world would use the flag, for example, in Russia, Mexico and Japan. In 1919, Italian fascists adopted it too, and it became the symbol of neo-fascist movements in Europe. In France, black flags re-emerged in May 1968 among students. In the 21st century, Islamist political parties also made it their color, alluding to the black standard of the Abbasid dynasty, which ruled the Muslim world from 750 until 1258.

Red Is for Revolution

Red is the color of blood, battle, passion and hard-fought freedom. It was the color of standards used in 16th-century Germany during the jacqueries, which were large peasant rebellions. Red can also represent prohibition and repression. At the start of the French Revolution, in 1789, a red pennant deployed by the municipality signaled to the crowd to disperse before troops started firing on them. That did not prevent the French revolutionaries from adopting the red flag in 1793. During the uprising of June 5, 1832, red flags appeared in the processions of protesters and on the barricades with the words: "Liberty or Death." The red flag became associated with the people's fight for social justice and was subsequently outlawed in some European nations. In the spirit of power, a red flag symbolizes blood, struggle and chaos. Although it was for a time rivaled by the black flag, red won the day among labor and grassroots movements in the mid-19th century. It became the official symbol of the International Workingmen's Association, born in London in 1854. It subsequently symbolized trade unions and internationalism. After the Russian Revolution, it became the standard for communism, as demonstrated by the flags of various communist countries, including China, Vietnam and the USSR.

"The red flag trembled in the air, moving to the right and to the left, then rose again." »

Mother, Maxim Gorky

3

national flags
out of 4 contain red.

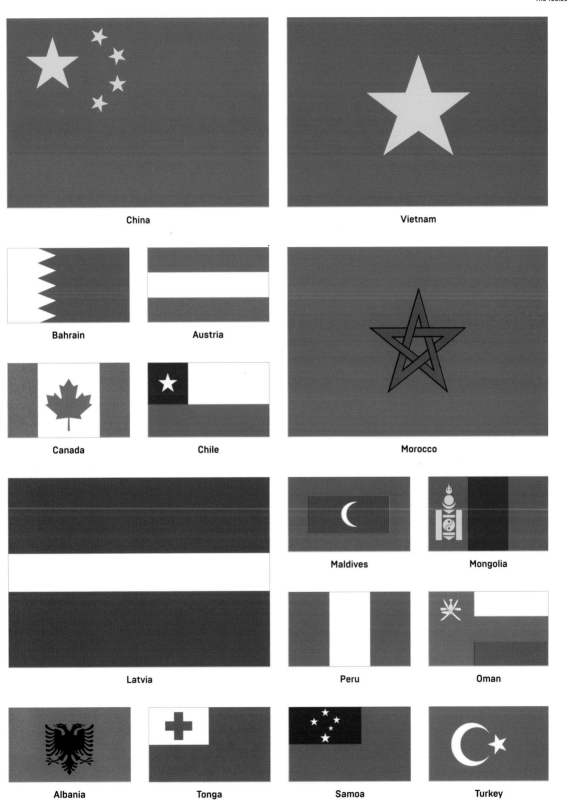

China

Vietnam

Bahrain

Austria

Canada

Chile

Morocco

Maldives

Mongolia

Latvia

Peru

Oman

Albania

Tonga

Samoa

Turkey

Micronesia

Blue Is for Sky, Sea, the Horizon and Hope

Sky blue is the color of the United Nations flag because of its associations with hope. This blue is echoed on the flag of Somalia, a country born through the intervention of the United Nations. The Argentinian flag, with its two horizontal bands of light blue framing a white band, served as a model for many other Latin American countries. Its famous "celestial" blue was not as light on the original flag, but it was gradually lightened to make it stand out from the more intense blue of the Bourbons and became the symbol of independence. Blue can hold a variety of meanings, but it mainly represents the sea — and quite aptly so for the flags of Honduras, Nicaragua and Guatemala, three countries surrounded by two oceans.

Guatemala

Argentina

Somalia

Kazakhstan

Botswana

Democratic Republic of the Congo

Natural Blue

The flag of Botswana refers a great deal to nature: Blue symbolizes the rain (the country's motto *Pula* literally means "rain"), and the black band and two white bands refer to the country's national animal, the zebra.

Nicaragua

Greece

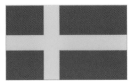

Sweden

Honduras

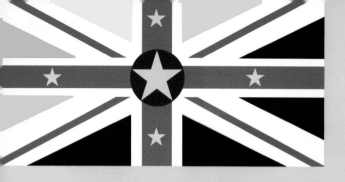

Niue

Yellow Is for Sun, Gold and Wisdom

The color of the sun and gold, yellow symbolizes heat, wealth and hope. It is often evocative of the nation's monarchy, such as on the flags of Bhutan, Brazil, Brunei and Spain. In Barbados, yellow refers to the sand. It is also used to represent the sun (Grenada), wheat fields (Lithuania and Ukraine) as well as gold and other mineral wealth (many South American countries, including Bolivia, Colombia and Ecuador, and African countries, such as Benin, Central African Republic and Guinea).

Brunei

Ukraine

Bhutan

Spain

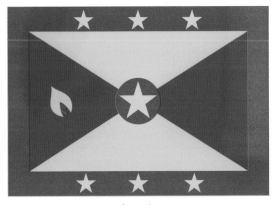

Grenada

Colombia

Ecuador

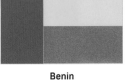

Benin

Vatican City

Saint Vincent and the
Grenadines

Bangladesh

Green Is for Nature and Islam

Green exemplifies vegetation, fertile lands and agriculture. On the flag of Bangladesh (above) it symbolizes the vitality of the country's agricultural land. In the West, it is the color of luck and hope as well as moderation, since it is found at the center of a rainbow and the color wheel. In the Koran, green represents paradise and immortality. According to Muslim tradition, it is the favorite color of the prophet Muhammad; it is said that his banner was green with a gold braid. The Ottoman Empire reclaimed this color for its religious flag. Today, green is found on the flags of most Arab and Muslim countries.

1

The flag of Dominica is the only national flag that contains purple.

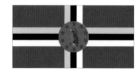

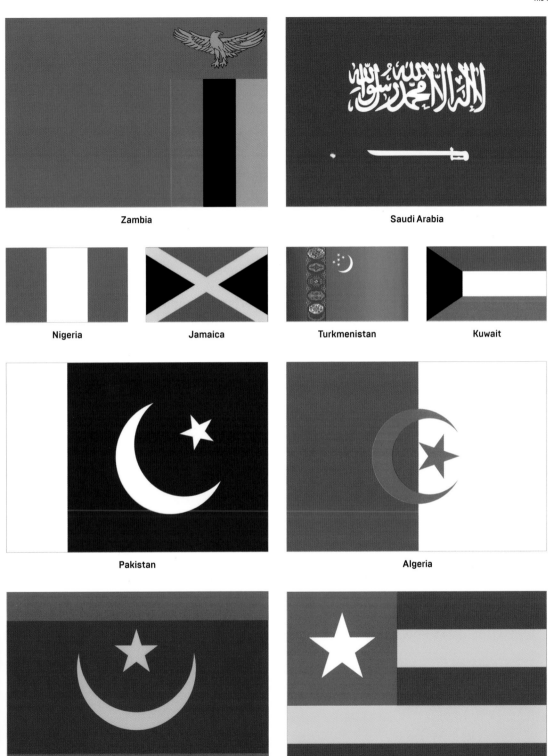

Zambia

Saudi Arabia

Nigeria

Jamaica

Turkmenistan

Kuwait

Pakistan

Algeria

Mauritania

Togo

GEOMETRY AS A SYMBOL

In addition to colors, flags often incorporate geometric patterns that make them more recognizable at a distance. The patterns are usually quite simple, but there are many variations.

Horizontal or vertical stripes, crosses, diagonal lines, circles, squares, triangles and so on — on a flag, geometric shapes become symbols. Motifs are sometimes added to the center or the canton. In some cases, the shapes and colors reflect those of the blazon or coat of arms of a founding figure or dynasty. On others, they symbolize nature and the country's resources. They can also be associated with moral values. The messages can also sometimes be combined, and there are multiple shapes that converge to form flags that are at times very complex — and all the more interesting to decode. To represent its people, every nation makes use of geometry, from simple shapes (rectangles, circles, triangles) to more complex motifs (suns, crosses, stars).

49

That is the number of squares on the Wiphala flag (at right), which is an emblem of the Indigenous peoples of the Andes. It bears a seven-by-seven square patchwork of seven different colors.

530 RECTANGLES
(including stripes) in total on national flags

19 CROSSES

14 CRESCENT MOONS

19 SUNS

14 CIRCLES

83 TRIANGLES
in total

92 STARS
in total

**79 IRREGULAR
POLYGONS**

Horizontal Stripes: Coming Together

The stacking of horizontal stripes can symbolize that a country was built in successive steps, thanks to peoples' associations, regions assembling and collective values. Stripes of matching width illustrate equality and stability, while stripes of unequal size suggest a hierarchy, emphasizing a theme or serving as a background for an emblem.

Flags with three horizontal stripes are by far the most common design (44% of national flags), but certain flags have considerably more stripes (13 for the United States and 14 for Malaysia). The Republic of Poland has two stripes: white on top and red on the bottom, commemorating the heraldic colors of the 11th-century Kingdom of Poland.

76
flags
out of the 201 national flags have horizontal stripes.

11
flags
have 2 horizonal stripes

50
flags
have 3 horizonal stripes

Poland

Lithuania

The three stripes of the Lithuanian flag, adopted in 1989, reflect the colors of the coat of arms of Władysław II of Poland, grand duke of Lithuania in the 14th century: yellow, green and red. However, the young republic also wanted to associate other symbols to those colors: the sun, wheat fields and prosperity with yellow; nature and hope with green; and land and bloodshed in the name of liberty with red.

Uganda

The flag of Uganda has six horizontal stripes and takes its colors — black, yellow and red — from the flag of the Uganda People's Congress, a political party that actively fought for the country's independence. The six horizontal stripes of equal width represent the three colors of Pan-Africanism. In the center, set against a white circle, is the country's emblem: a gray crowned crane with a yellow and red crest and a red and white wing, symbolizing prosperity. To Ugandans, those colors also symbolize the people of Africa: sun and bloodshed in the name of liberty.

2
flags
have 4 horizonal stripes

Mauritius

11
flags
have 5 horizontal stripes

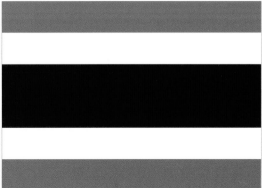

Thailand

Vertical Stripes: Breaking Apart

22

flags

have three vertical stripes, but on six of those flags the stripes are only in two colors.

75%

of flags

have three vertical stripes.

Orientation of Stripes

Romania changed the orientation of its flag's blue, yellow and red stripes — which were originally horizontal but are now vertical — in honor of the three historical regions that make up the country: Transylvania, Walachia and Moldavia.

Vertical stripes give a certain dynamism to a flag. They often mark a turning point in a country's history. For example, the French tricolor flag remains the model for a revolution that gives birth to a democracy. Many countries were subsequently inspired to affirm their ideas of liberty and democracy. Thus, the flag of Chad is largely inspired by the French tricolor flag because it was chosen by the last governor of the former French colony of Chad. It was adopted after the country's independence, in 1959, and represents sky and water (blue), sun and Saharan sand (gold) and the sacrifices of the people (red). It is very similar to the flags of Romania, Andorra and Moldova. On the latter two flags, a coat of arms appears on the center yellow stripe; the Romanian flag also had its coat of arms on the center stripe of its flag at one time, but it was removed in 1959. All three flags do, however, use lighter shades of blue than the indigo of the Chad flag.

Other countries chose vertical stripes to level the playing field among the peoples or regions that make it up. Flags with three vertical stripes were first flown in Ireland in 1830, to celebrate the return of the tricolor flag in France after the July Revolution of 1830. The Republic of Ireland's green, white and orange tricolor flag first appeared in 1848, when it was adopted by the revolutionary and nationalist Young Ireland movement, and it was flown again during the Easter Rising of 1916. It symbolizes political and religious liberation from the Crown of England.

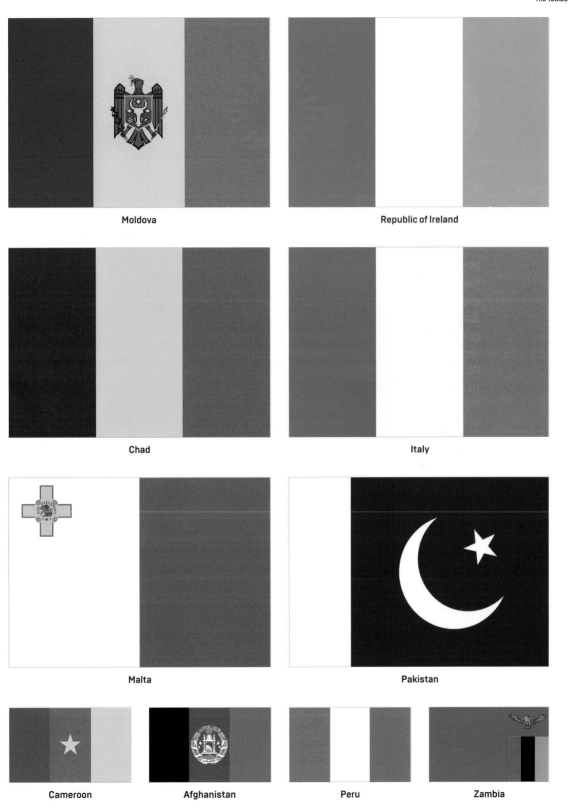

Moldova

Republic of Ireland

Chad

Italy

Malta

Pakistan

Cameroon

Afghanistan

Peru

Zambia

Circles: Sun and Moon

Most countries that choose a circle for their flag want to echo the sun. The flag of Japan, through its simplicity, is a great example. Very similar is the flag of the People's Republic of Bangladesh, which has a red circle depicting the sun on a green background. It illustrates a poem by Rabindranath Tagore: "O Sun, rise upon the bleeding hearts blossoming in flowers morning, and the torchlight revelry of pride shrunken to ashes." This poem recalls the country's hostilities with Pakistan that led to the independence of Bengal in 1971, which is symbolized by red, for the color of the blood shed by the people of Bangladesh. Green represents the vitality of the youth and agricultural land. The circle is not centered on the flag but sits instead toward the left, closer to the flagpole. However, when the flag flies in the wind, the circle appears centered thanks to an optical illusion.

The flag of the Republic of Niger bears an orange circle that symbolizes both the sun and the battles led by the Nigerian people for their country. The stripes represent the Sahara, which lies in the north of the country (orange), the fertile region of the Niger Basin in the south (green) and the savanna (white). Niger's flag also represents the country's motto: fraternity, work, progress.

The circle on the flag of Palau, like that of Bangladesh, is not centered. The yellow circle on a blue background represents not the sun but the full moon, an emblem of peace and love, silhouetted against the Pacific Ocean. This symbol is also an allusion to human activities like fishing, farming and festivals celebrating the full moon.

> **"O Sun, rise upon the bleeding hearts blossoming in flowers morning, and the torchlight revelry of pride shrunken to ashes."**
> Rabindranath Tagore

Japan

According to legend, the solar disk refers to the Shinto sun goddess Amaterasu, ancestor of a 13th-century emperor of Japan. This symbol of divinity was said to protect the empire against the Mongols. It also represents the country as "the origin of the sun" (see page 112).

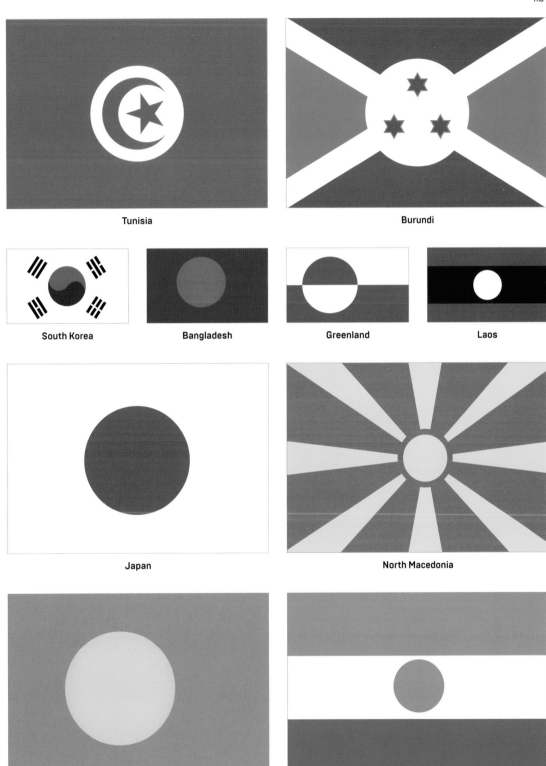

Tunisia

Burundi

South Korea

Bangladesh

Greenland

Laos

Japan

North Macedonia

Palau

Niger

Triangles: Standing Out

Most flags that have a triangle feature that triangle on the hoist. On certain flags, the triangles are solid and set against a striped background. On others, the triangles bear a symbol or emblem. Triangles also sometimes split the flag in two, overlap each other or extend into a Y shape. In some cases, there are multiple triangles that occupy the entire flag (Eritrea). While others are formed by lines or stripes that divide the flag into two or more triangles (Marshall Islands and Seychelles).

A triangle on the hoist gives a flag a strong visual identity. Such a design combines multiple colors in a more original way than stripes. For example, the large isosceles triangle on the hoist of the Czech Republic's flag helps it stand out from other flags that use the same Pan-Slavic colors (blue, white and red). The same can also be said of the flags of Sudan, Palestine and Jordan, which play around with a combination Pan-Arabic colors (black, white, green and red) using the same structure (three horizontal stripes of the same width and a triangle on the hoist). The flag of the Bahamas is composed of three horizontal stripes: aquamarineon the top of bottom, for the ocean, and gold in the center for the islands' sand. The black equilateral triangle positioned near the flagpole side represents the country's unity: Christopher Columbus disembarked on the Bahamian island of San Salvador in 1492, and privateers founded the Republic of Pirates on New Providence Island, which flew a black flag with a skull and crossbones from 1706 to 1718. The black triangle represents this period in the Bahamas' history.

Layers of History

The flag of the Democratic Republic of East Timor features two overlapping triangles on a red background, to symbolize the country's fight to gain its independence. The black equilateral triangle refers to the dark times in the country's history, and the yellow isosceles triangle evokes its colonial past. The white star represents the peace and light that guides the people.

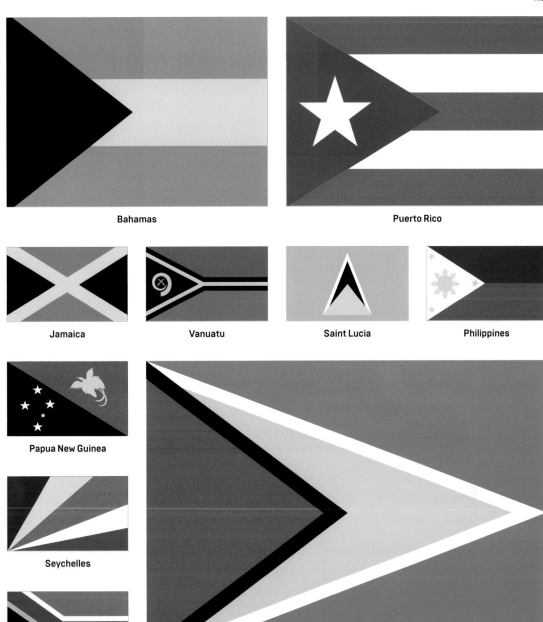

Bahamas

Puerto Rico

Jamaica

Vanuatu

Saint Lucia

Philippines

Papua New Guinea

Seychelles

South Africa

Guyana

Eritrea

The Golden Arrow

That is the nickname of Guyana's flag, in reference to its central yellow triangle. All of this flag's colors are associated with the country's natural resources (green for forests, yellow for mineral resources and white for rivers) and the qualities of the Guyanese people (red for energy and black for perseverance).

Crosses

Crosses are found on many flags, not only because they can be used to divide spaces in various esthetically pleasing ways, but also because they are a strong Christian symbol. Crosses were used on clothing and on some standards during the Crusades to the Holy Land in the 11th and 12th centuries.

During that time, French crusaders waved a red cross on a white background, while the English bore a white cross on a red background, the Flemish a green cross on a white background and the Italians a yellow cross on a white background. The colors changed over time, and, during the Hundred Years' War (1337–1453), the English adopted the red cross of Saint George on a white background and the French troops adopted the white cross of Saint Michael on a blue background, which are the color of Saint Martin's robes. Today, there are 27 different types of crosses. The most common are the Saint George's Cross and Saint Andrew's Cross, or crux decussata, which generally appear on flags in an X shape, called "saltire" in heraldry.

Most Nordic countries copied the Danish flag and chose an off-center Greek cross. To create the optical illusion of centeredness, the vertical arm is shifted toward the flagpole and the horizontal arm is extended toward the fly end. Off-center crosses are referred to as "Scandinavian" because they are featured on the flags of Scandinavian countries (like Denmark, Sweden and Norway), but the also appear on the flags of other Nordic countries (like Finland, the Faroe Islands and Åland Islands) as well as several British Isles. The origin of the Scandinavian cross is attributed to the Baltic Crusades. In 1219, the king of Denmark saw lightning in the shape of a cross in the sky ahead of his victory at the Battle of Lyndanisse against non-Christian Estonians. Considered a divine protection, this cross would later be used by the Kalmar Union, a confederation that reunited the Kingdoms of Sweden, Denmark and Norway between 1397 and 1523.

29

flags

have at least one cross.

Saint George's Cross

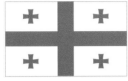

Georgia

England

Saint Andrew's Cross

Scotland

Jamaica

Tenerife

Greek cross

Greece

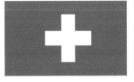

Switzerland

Georgian cross

Malta

The Scandinavian Cross

This cross appears on the flags of seven countries and autonomous regions in Northern Europe. It should more accurately be called the "Nordic cross" because, in a strict sense, Denmark, Norway and Sweden are the only Scandinavian counties. The flags of some of the British Isles that have both Nordic and Gaelic heritages also use this cross.

Faroe Islands

Orkney Islands

County of Caithness

Sweden

Denmark

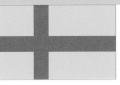

Kalmar Union

THE BLAZON

In the Middle Ages, heraldic devices such as blazons were used on knights' shields to more easily identify them in battle and tournaments. On the flags of today, this symbol, new or old, is always associated with nation-building.

Coats of arms became widespread in the 13th century, when their use on fabrics became regulated. As such, only kings, princes and emperors had the right to bear a standard, which is a long, triangular piece of fabric with two tails, or a square banner adorned with their coat of arms. Marquesses, counts, viscounts and barons bore rectangular banners that were taller than they were wide, while knights used a triangular pennant. Until the 14th century, their decoration was limited to heraldry, but they later became personalized. The colors represented warrior qualities and moral values, while graphics and adornments told the story of a family, town or province that played a major role in the creation of state, evolving according to alliances and military feats.

Whether it is simple or, more often, a composite image divided into sections, a coat of arms features highly codified geometric motifs and "accessories," such as humans (Belize), animals (Serbia, Moldova, Montenegro), vegetation (Fiji, Ecuador, Equatorial Guinea), celestial bodies (Croatia), crosses (Slovakia, Dominican Republic) or weapons (Guatemala). A country's motto, as well as its national symbol, is often associated with its blazon.

Honoring the Blazon

Poland does not portray its coat of arms on its flag, but the signification is retained through colors: white for the eagle spreading its wings and red for the sunset on the shield.

Spain's Blazon

Spain's flag is one of the finest examples of a composite blazon. It has six different coats of arms that illustrates the building of the kingdom: Castile's castle, León's lion, Aragon's red and gold stripes, Navarre's gold chains, Granada's pomegranate and the fleur-de-lis of the Bourbon-Anjou dynasty.

Ecuador

Andorra

Serbia

Croatia

Slovakia

Moldova

Equatorial Guinea

Belize

Guatemala

Portugal

Mexico

Brunei

Fiji

San Marino

Montenegro

El Salvador

Tajikistan

Haiti

Slovenia

Nicaragua

Vatican City

Harvard
University

City of Paris

Real Madrid

Great Seal of the
United States

THE IMPORTANCE OF NATURE

While concrete depictions of nature are relatively rare on national flags (12%), elements of nature are often represented in more discreet ways, particularly through colors and patterns.

Nature is often represented with stripes of colors: blue for the sea, green for forests, yellow for sand (Bahamas) or agriculture, white for snow (Lebanon). Geometric shapes are also used: triangles can represent mountains or volcanoes, and stars are used in the place of islands. In contrast, plants delicately woven through a coat of arms can represent concepts or heritage: sheaves of grain evoke agricultural wealth, and a laurel or olive branch can be a symbol of victory or peace.

There are countless subjects tied to nature that appear on flags through a wide variety of idyllic landscapes, colorful trees and flowers, and ripe agricultural products. Some genuinely resemble postcards aimed at attracting tourists and promoting the region. Ecuador offers a good example of a flag focused on nature and natural resources: yellow evokes gold and agriculture (bananas, corn, barley and wheat), and blue represents the sky and ocean. The national blazon in the center shows a landscape of the Guayas River flowing through the plains at the foot of the snow-covered Chimborazo Volcano. Volcanoes are commonly featured on flags — there are five on El Salvador's flag! The one on Reunion Island's flag, Piton de la Fournaise, an active 8,635-foot (2,632 m) volcano, is represented in a stylized fashion. Mountains are often used in the background and give dimension to flags, like on the flags of Slovakia, certain Canadian provinces, certain Japanese prefectures, Indonesia, Mongolia, and regions in Latin American — countries that are home to the highest mountain ranges in the world.

Double Emblem

Nature is featured both on the flag and in the national motto's of Canada and Belize. Canada's motto, *a Mari usque ad Mare* (From sea to sea), reflects the vastness of its territory, while Belize's motto, *sub Umbra Floreo* (Under the shade I flourish), symbolizes the country's strength.

5 Stripes, 5 Seas

The blue stripes of the Greek flag represent the five seas that surround it (Ionian Sea, Mediterranean Sea, Sea of Crete, Aegean Sea and Thracian Sea).

SUN

SEA

FOREST, VEGETATION

MOUNTAINS/VOLCANOES

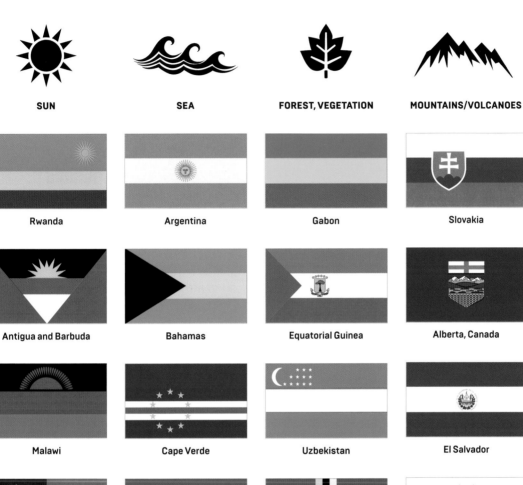

Rwanda

Argentina

Gabon

Slovakia

Antigua and Barbuda

Bahamas

Equatorial Guinea

Alberta, Canada

Malawi

Cape Verde

Uzbekistan

El Salvador

Republic of China (Taiwan)

Honduras

Dominica

Toyama, Japan

North Macedonia

Kiribati

Eritrea

Slovenia

Animals: Quite the Menagerie!

While a bevy of animals — with fur, feathers, scales and shells — can be found on the flags of states, provinces and dependent territories, they are rarer on national flags. Nevertheless, their presence always retains a strong symbolic meaning.

The eagle, whether perched, in flight or double-headed, can evoke power, such as on the flags of Moldova and Mexico, as well as prestige and liberty, such as on the flag of Zambia. Montenegro's flag has a double-headed eagle and a lion, which are both imperial animals. The lion on the backside of the Paraguayan flag is designed in a realistic manner, while Spain chose a rampant lion straight out of heraldry. The golden lion on the Sri Lankan flag is statuesque, almost deified: its sword represents the strength and sovereignty of the nation, its curly mane represents wisdom and meditation, its beard symbolizes pure language and its nose represents intelligence. Previously, an elephant reigned on the flag of Ceylon. Known for its wisdom and intelligence, this animal appears on the flags of several African and Asian countries, but it disappeared with decolonization. Similarly, animals from heraldry, like the lion, leopard, horse, deer and bear, are now more widespread on regional flags than on national flags. The exceptions are the flags of the 14 British Overseas Territories whose coats of arms predominantly feature nature with a rich and varied bestiary, including the turtle, lion, sheep, tern, albatross, plover, lobster, conch, macaroni penguin, elephant seal, reindeer, dolphin and the like — most of which, as it happens, are now species that warrant protection.

4

Animals

The flag of South Georgia and the South Sandwich Islands has four animals. Its coat of arms contains a rampant lion, a reindeer (on top), an elephant seal (the largest seal) and a macaroni penguin (a type of crested penguin). It's a real menagerie!

Moldova

Montenegro

Wales

Zambia

Mexico

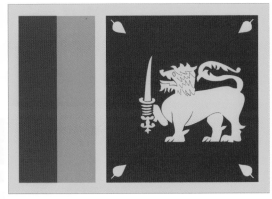

Sri Lanka

Papua New Guinea

Flowers and Other Plants

Flags are full of lush and varied vegetation that illustrates the natural resources of the relevant nation or region.

Some trees are displayed as the country's emblem. For example, Lebanon's cedar tree, which is a biblical symbol of eternity and peace; Canada's maple leaf, a true hymn to the environment; Equatorial Guinea's kapok tree (or silk cotton tree), a traditional species of Africa's rainforests; or Belize's mahogany tree, which is prized in furniture-making, among other industries. Characteristic of the Mediterranean coast and a sign of peace, the olive tree is featured on many flags. It is often reduced to a branch and is sometimes combined with a laurel wreath — a stylish way of showing that a peaceful nation nonetheless knows how to wage war and can defeat its adversaries if attacked.

More colorful than trees, there are countless flowers designed in a variety of ways, both stylized and realistic. Some are an easy-to-identify species, such as the lotus, sunflower, rose or lily, while others are rare and little-known plants, such as the showy lady's slipper of Minnesota, a North American variety of orchid that can measure up to 3 feet (1 m) high. Many references to nature involve agricultural goods. For example, the vineyards and grapes of counties in Hungary, the wheat of Afghanistan and the rice and cotton of regions in Indonesia.

Under a Magnifying Glass

If you look closely, you can often see interesting tidbits on flags. For example, the flag of Grenada, an island nation in the Caribbean, nicknamed the "Isle of Spice," features nutmeg, and the pomegranate, which can be seen on Spain's coat of arms, represents the Spanish city of Granada.

Lebanon

Canada

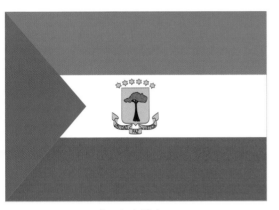

Equatorial Guinea

Belize

Minnesota

Hong Kong

Saint Vincent and the Grenadines

San Marino

Guatemala

Cyprus

WEAPONS

Weapons can be found on 15 national flags as well as on some regional flags.

There are more than 20 different types of arms featured on flags, including bladed weapons (scimitar, sword, saber, machete, ax), projectiles (bow and arrow, catapult), artillery (cannons) and firearms (rifle, machine gun, pistol). They are often seen in pairs, arranged symmetrically, as though laid down after a battle. Most have also lost their wartime function and gained peaceful and cultural value. All sorts of Indigenous weapons are a matter of pride for communities, such as the Omani *saif* and *khanjar*, worn on a belt, or the *kastane*, which is a short ceremonial saber of Sri Lanka and a symbol of sovereignty associated with the lion. Several regions in Indonesia display traditional weapons on their flags. The weapons become trophies, such as Haiti's cannons and Guatemala's rifles surrounded by a laurel crown, a symbol of victory. Mozambique's flag features an AK-47 assault rifle, which is a symbol of the people's fight for independence. In 2005, a contest was launched to change the flag, which is the only one that shows a modern-day firearm. However, this formidable weapon gives testimony to both the country's anti-colonial struggles and its civil war, and the people chose to keep this symbol, which they associate with liberty.

15
national flags feature weapons:

3
have swords

3
have sabers

2
have rifles

1
has cannons

1
has a trident

Oman

Angola

Guatemala

Barbados

Dominican Republic

Haiti

Saudi Arabia

4

national flags have spears

The spears arranged horizontally behind the Zulu shield of the Kingdom of Eswatini are symbols of power and peace between black and white peoples. The spears of Kenya crossed behind the Maasai shield refers to both the defense of liberty and the father of Kenya's independence, whose name, Jomo Kenyatta, translates to "burning spear of Kenya."

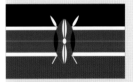

Kenya

Swaziland

Ecuador

RELIGIOUS SYMBOLS

Over the centuries, many countries have proudly proclaimed their religion on their flags using simple but powerful symbols, such as geometric shapes and colors.

The Star of David symbolizes Judaism. On the flag of Israel, it appears between two blue stripes against a white background that evoke the tallit, the Jewish prayer shawl.

Christianity is represented by different crosses. For Denmark, Finland and Iceland, where the Lutheran Protestant church is the official church, the cross is off-center and extends across the entire flag. On the flag of Greece, where the Orthodox church dominates, the cross is square (the Greek cross) and symbolizes the country's religious conversion to Christianity in the 4th century. On the flag of the Vatican, an absolute monarchy headed by the pope, a cross adorns the papal tiara and the keys of Saint Peter. On Georgia's flag, a large Saint George's Cross is combined with four small heraldic crosses (Orthodox).

Islam, the religion with the widest presence on national flags, is represented by colors (green for paradise, black and white for the prophet's standards and red for the Hashemite dynasty, former rulers of Mecca) and by two main symbols, the crescent moon and the five-pointed star. Borrowed from the Ottoman Empire, these motifs represent the end of Ramadan and the five pillars of Islam. Certain Muslim flags feature professions of the Islamic faith (*Shahada*) or the *Takbir* (*Allahu akbar*, which means "Allah is greater than everything").

Buddhist symbols primarily include the yin and yang, seen on the flags of South Korea and Mongolia; the sacred fig leaves, under whose shade Buddha mediated, which appear on the four corners of the Sri Lankan flag; and the colors orange, saffron and gold, which are an expression of purity, wisdom and renunciation.

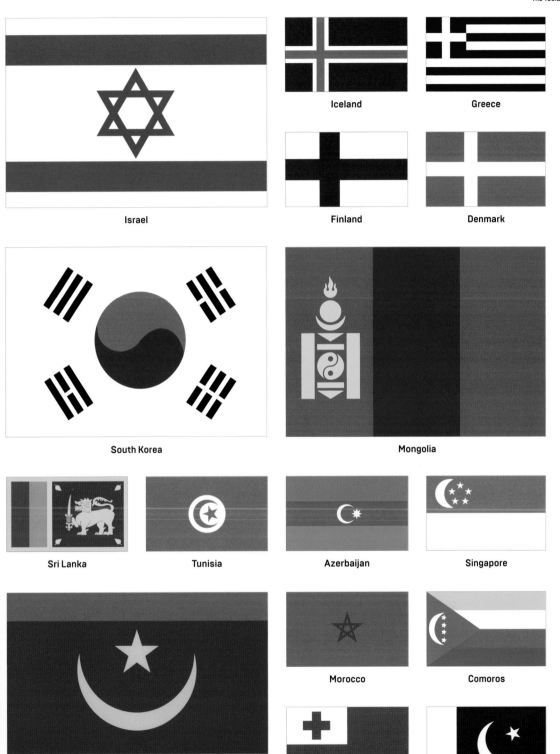

Iceland

Greece

Israel

Finland

Denmark

South Korea

Mongolia

Sri Lanka

Tunisia

Azerbaijan

Singapore

Mauritania

Morocco

Comoros

Tonga

Pakistan

(RE) CONSTRUCTING THE PAST

The history of national flags is inherently linked with the history of other regional flags. A flag is born with a nation, becomes the symbol of that nation and follows its political evolution. Sometimes a flag remains unchanged, while others transform with time, as the borders and governments of the nation change. A flag may even perish, either because the country disappears or is absorbed by another country or because a country breaks apart into multiple nations. In that case, a new flag is created soon after and history begins anew.

THE RECOGNITION OF A STATE

The birth of a flag almost always signifies the disappearance of one or several others. The history of the 20th century could be told through flags.

In 1920, the League of Nations (LN) developed an official proposed list of the world's states, which identified 85 sovereign or separatist states seeking international recognition, including Canada, Australia, New Zealand and South Africa, which at that time were part of the British Empire. In 2012, the number of sovereign states recognized by the UN had more than doubled because of decolonization and the collapse of large empires like the Ottoman Empire and the USSR. Former countries regained their sovereignty, while others won theirs — and they all had new flags. There are also many countries whose sovereignty is disputed. Some are recognized by the UN, but not necessarily by all its members. Others are not recognized by the UN but are still members. A few are independent or de facto autonomies but are not recognized by the UN, like several regions in Somalia that are controlled by local leaders. For all, however, a flag is the first step toward independence. In 1946, the UN established a list of 74 non-self-governing territories that the organization deemed "non-decolonized" and for which they recommend independence. In 2018, there were still 17 territories on that list.

1789
More than 300 sovereign states
exist in Europe.

1920
67 sovereign states
exist in the world according to the League of Nations, including 43 member states and 18 non-recognized states.

2020
193 nations
are UN members and two countries are observer states (Vatican City and Palestine).

68

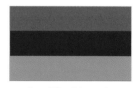

Republic of Armenia

People's Republic of China

Cyprus

Republic of Korea

People's Republic of Korea

Israel

Diplomatic Struggles

Certain territories are not recognized as a sovereign state even though they claim to be. They may or may not be UN members, and their independence is likely disputed by one or more states. For example, the Republic of Somaliland is not recognized by any other state. At stake is a diplomatic standoff regarding the territory's independence.

Abkhazia

Sahrawi Arab Democratic Republic

Republic of China (Taiwan)

Turkish Republic of Northern Cyprus

Kosovo

South Ossetia

Palestine

Republic of Somaliland

Transnistria (Pridnestrovian Moldavian Republic)

Donetsk People's Republic

Luhansk People's Republic

Nagorno-Karabakh Republic

Western Sahara

Anguilla

Bermuda

British Virgin Islands

Cayman Islands

Falkland Islands (Malvinas Islands)

Monserrat

Saint Helena

Turks and Caicos

United States Virgin Islands

Gibraltar

America Samoa

French Polynesia

New Caledonia

Aspiring to Autonomy... or Not

The list of 17 non-self-governing territories (which include some British Overseas Territories) compiled by the UN is a subject of controversy because certain countries, such as Western New Guinea and Tibet, are not included. In contrast, the inhabitants of some of the territories on the list voted against independence, such as Tokelau Islands, a territory of New Zealand; the Falkland Islands, a British Overseas Territory; and French Polynesia.

Guam

Pitcairn

Tokelau Islands

THE OLDEST FLAGS

Among the flags that are still used today, there are several contenders for the title of world's oldest flag. However, with legend and history so closely intertwined, it is difficult to name a winner.

According to legend, the oldest flag in the world belongs to Scotland, one of the United Kingdom's constituent nations. Its flag features the Saint Andrew's Cross (white on a blue background), which is called a "saltire" in heraldry. It symbolizes the instrument of the eponymous martyr, who is Scotland's patron saint. This flag is said to have been born in 832, when King Óengus II, king of the Picts and a Scottish ally, defeated the Saxons. He looked up and saw a saltire in the shape of the clouds in the blue sky.

The oldest national flag still in use is Denmark's — a red background with a white cross. It has never been modified since its creation, which dates back to 1219, according to legend. The red background adopts the colors of the Normans' banners and represents bloodshed. Nicknamed Dannebrog (which means "Danish cloth" or "red cloth"), this flag is a symbol of Danish identity and is used for all national and family celebrations. Shifted to the hoist side, the Scandinavian cross, symbol of the Crusades, is found on the flags of Sweden, Norway, Finland, Iceland, the Faroe Islands and the Åland Islands.

The Austrian and Latvian flags were also created in the 13th century. They were modified several times before their original shapes and colors were restored. Netherlands's flag, created in 1572, changed colors from orange to red. Then, at the beginning of the 19th century, a number of new flags emerged, such as the United Kingdom's flag, which was created in 1801; Argentina's flag, created in 1812 and officially recognized in 1816; Chile's flag, adopted on October 18, 1817, a few months before the country's official independence; and France's flag, which was adopted in 1830.

1219
Denmark

According to legend, on June 15, 1219, King Valdemar the Victorious was suffering a bitter defeat in his Crusade in present-day Estonia when a banner with a white cross on a red background fell from the sky. Luck turned in favor of the Danes, who won the battle.

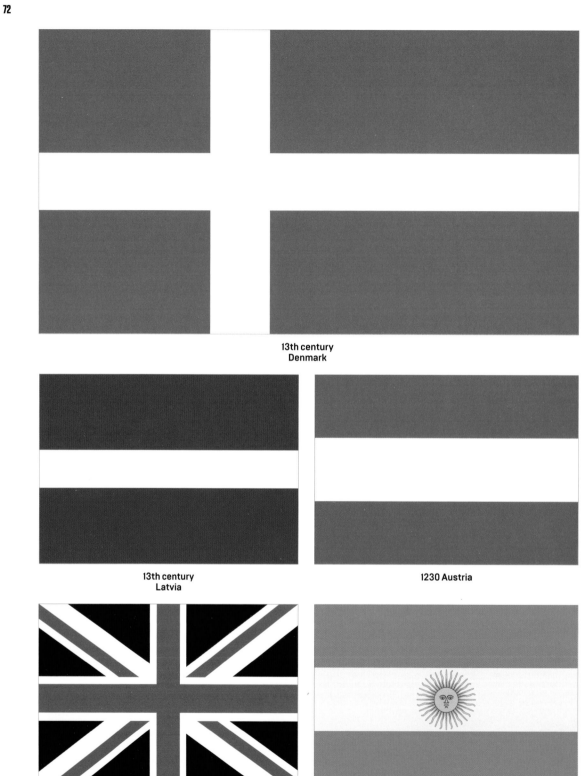

13th century
Denmark

13th century
Latvia

1230 Austria

1801
United Kingdom

1812
Argentina

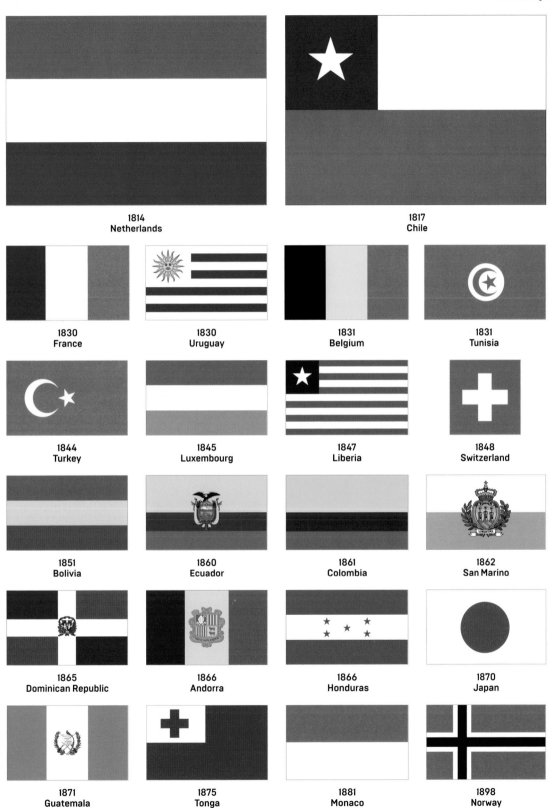

1814
Netherlands

1817
Chile

1830
France

1830
Uruguay

1831
Belgium

1831
Tunisia

1844
Turkey

1845
Luxembourg

1847
Liberia

1848
Switzerland

1851
Bolivia

1860
Ecuador

1861
Colombia

1862
San Marino

1865
Dominican Republic

1866
Andorra

1866
Honduras

1870
Japan

1871
Guatemala

1875
Tonga

1881
Monaco

1898
Norway

THE BIRTH OF A FLAG

The birth of a new state goes hand in hand with the creation of a new flag. Whether they were created after a victory or defeat or following a change of dynasty or political regime, all new countries need an emblem to unite their people.

The first flags were used on battlefields; however, they are often given legendary, even divine origins. For example, the Danish flag is said to have fallen from the sky during a battle in 1219.

Today, the birth of a flag signifies the death of one or several others. The process generally involves either a consultation within the party in power or a contest, which is often organized by a marketing or ad agency that makes an initial selection. The winners are then chosen by a committee made up of politicians, artists, communications and marketing professionals and, in rare cases, citizens. The final decision is approved by a government vote.

Other flags were born of private initiatives but had a national destiny. For example, the idea for the Armenian flag began in Paris. In 1885, Armenian students wanted to attend the funeral of Victor Hugo while waving a flag. However, the Armenian flag no longer existed, since the country had been divided between Persia and the Ottoman Empire. At their request, Armenian Catholic priest Ghevont Alishan designed the tricolor flag with red, green and white horizontal stripes, in a nod to the colors of the Orthodox Easter holiday.

Austrian Flag

The Austrian flag represents the bloody tunic worn by Duke Leopold V, who was hurt in the Siege of Acre in 1191, during Crusades. The flag's white stripe represents the section of the duke's tunic that would have been under his belt, which would have been untouched by blood.

Armenian Flag

In 1918, Armenia gained independence. Its new red, blue and apricot flag uses the colors of the dynasty that reigned over the Kingdom of Cilicia (or Lesser Armenia) from the 11th to 13th centuries. It was revived in 1990.

The original flag of New Zealand

Voting for Their Flag

In 2016, there were serious talks in New Zealand about changing the national flag — via a contest and voting. The Commonwealth nation has a flag derived from the Blue Ensign, a British state ensign that reproduces the Union Jack in the upper-left corner on a blue background, combined with the Southern Cross constellation, a symbol of the southern hemisphere.

Australia

The flag of New Zealand was created in 1869 and became official in 1902. Since the end of the 20th century, the question of whether it should be changed has been hotly debated. In 2014, then-Prime minister John Key decided to hold various referendums that would provide the opportunity to free the country of the colonial symbol that the Union Jack represents and better distinguish New Zealand's flag from the very similar Australian flag.

The selected flag

In 2015, the people of New Zealand cast the first votes to choose their favorite of five proposed flags (the selection committee received more than 10,000 entries). They chose a design that combined the Southern Cross and silver fern, which are both national symbols, on a black and blue background. However, during the March 2016 referendum, when New Zealanders voted between the new and former flags, 56.6% voted in favor of the existing flag.

10,292
proposals
were submitted to the selection committee.

40
Flags
From all the entries, the initial selection consisted of 40 "serious" flags (see following pages).

Wa kainga/Home

Land on the Long White
Cloud (Ocean Blue)

Land on the Long White
Cloud (Traditional Blue)

Huihui/Together

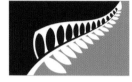

Silver Fern (Black and Silver)

New Zealand Matariki

Manawa (Blue and Green)

Unity Koru

Silver Fern (Black and White)

Tukutuku

Raranga

Koru and Stars

Inclusive

Koru Fin

Modern Hundertwasser Koru

Silver Fern (Green)

Curly Koru

Unity Koru

New Southern Cross

NZ One

Silver Fern (Black, White and Blue)

Silver Fern (Red, White and Blue)

Black Jack

Southern Koru

Pikopiko

Silver Fern (Black with Red Stars)

Southern Cross Horizon

Red Peak

Moving Forward

Finding Unity in Community

Silver Fern (Black and White)

The Seven Stars of Matariki

Embrace (Red and Blue)

Fern (Green, Black and White)

Silver Fern (Black, White and Red)

Koru (Black)

White and Black Fern

Manawa (Black and Green)

Koru (Blue)

Unity Fern (Red and Blue)

THE DEATH OF A FLAG

Countries often change flags. Though numerous, the reasons for such changes generally boil down to politics.

More often than not, a change of flag marks a change of regime. For example, when the Imperial State of Iran became an Islamic republic in 1979, it changed its flag to replace the imperial lion with a symbol of Islam. A change of flag can also mark that a country has achieved independence. The emblem of colonization on South Africa's flag disappeared along with apartheid in 1994 in favor of five colors that reflect the country's diversity. Zimbabwe (formerly Rhodesia) gained independence in 1980. In a little over a year, the country underwent no less than three changes: political regime, name and flag. It subsequently became an independent state recognized by the UN. Its new flag bears a red Marxist star; the colors of the ZANU-PF party (Zimbabwe African National Union), black, red, yellow and green, which was the party in power; and Zimbabwe's historical bird emblem.

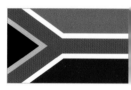

South Africa

The emblem of colonization disappeared from South Africa's flag along with apartheid in 1994 in favor of five colors that reflect the country's diversity.

32
flags
for the United States

24
flags
for Afghanistan

17
flags
for Venezuela

15
flags
for Azerbaijan

A change of flag can also be a political affirmation. For example, in 2004 in Georgia, the five-cross flag of the United National Movement, the party of President Saakachvili, was adopted when he came to power. The flag was chosen by parliament following a contest. In 1989 and again in 2010 in Myanmar, the Burmese military junta decided to give the country a new name, a new anthem and new flag.

Sometimes, a change of flag responds to a simple aesthetical preference. For example, the central coat of arms on the Paraguayan flag was simplified in 2013, and the lion, a symbol of peace and justice, on its back side resumed its original position, seated and facing the flag post. Sometimes public pressure encourages change, like in New Zealand, whose flag ultimately failed to change in 2016. Flags of certain countries have gone through dozens of versions (see below).

14
flags
for Moldova

13
flags
for the Philippines

12
flags
for Saudi Arabia

1
flag
for Denmark

The Collapse of the USSR

The Red Star

Its five points represent either the five classes of society or workers from across the five continents.

Hammer

The symbol of the proletariat, it represents industrial workers.

Sickle

It represents peasants and agricultural workers. It replaced the plow on the original emblem.

From 1922 to 1991, the Union of Soviet Socialist Republics brought together 15 states under one heavily symbolic flag: the red background, the color of the communist party and the blood of revolutionary fighters; the hammer and sickle, emblems of the workers and peasants union; and the gold-bordered red star of the Red Army. Adopted in 1923, the flag was modified twice: in 1955 the hammer and sickle were shrunken slightly and redesigned, and in 1980 the colors were brightened. Throughout the USSR's entire existence, each Soviet Socialist Republic also had its own flag. Created after each republic's annexation to the USSR, the flags all follow the same scheme: red background, a hammer and sickle in the upper-left canton and one or more stripes of color, a subtle reference to the country's history. In 1991, the dissolution of the USSR marked the end of its flag, which was replaced by 15 new flags corresponding to the 15 countries that regained their independence. Today, nine of these countries are members of the Commonwealth of Independent States (CIS) under the leadership of the Russian Federation. The flags of those states are inspired by former designs. For its part, Russia ironically revived the white, blue and red flag of the Russian Empire, which incorporates the Pan-Slavic colors seen on the flags of many Eastern European countries.

Armenia

Azerbaijan

Belarus

Estonia

Georgia

Kazakhstan

Kyrgyzstan

Latvia

An Imposing Union

The territories of the USSR represented one-sixth
of the Earth's surface.

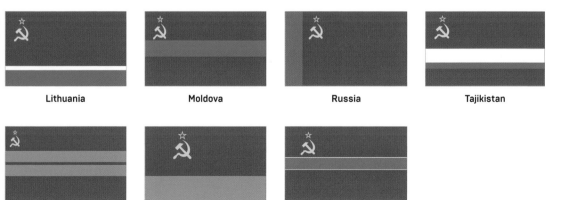

Lithuania	Moldova	Russia	Tajikistan

Turkmenistan	Ukraine	Uzbekistan

Commonwealth of Independent States

Post-USSR

The 15 states that made up the Soviet Union are currently all independent. Today, nine of them (marked with an asterisk) are reunited under one intergovernmental entity, the Commonwealth of Independent States, which is not legally recognized as an international organization.

Ukraine

Turkmenistan*

Uzbekistan*

Tajikistan*

Belarus*

Kyrgyzstan*

Moldova*

Armenia*

Azerbaijan*

Russian Federation*

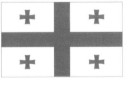

Georgia

Kazakhstan*

Estonia

Lithuania

Latvia

The Breakup of Yugoslavia

Yugoslavia had its beginnings in 1945. Its flag retained the Pan-Slavic colors of blue, white and red — the same colors of liberty and the French Revolution. However, a yellow-bordered red star was added to symbolize communist rule. From 1991, Slovenia, Croatia, Bosnia and Herzegovina, and Macedonia (present-day North Macedonia) gained their independence. In 1992, the Federal Republic of Yugoslavia, which was then made up of only Serbia and Montenegro, kept the colorsof the former Yugoslavian flag but dropped the red star. The other countries chose to keep a flag with blue, white and red — the Pan-Slavic colors— and added their coat of arms.

The Yugoslavian flag fell out of use completely when Montenegro gained independence in 2006. Serbia added its coat of arms to the flag, a double-headed eagle from the Serbian Nemanjić dynasty. Montenegro chose a red background with a double-headed eagle and a lion — the coat of arms of King Nicholas I of Montenegro — inspired by the flag that dominated the region between 1878 and 1910. Kosovo, which unilaterally declared itself independent in 2008, remained under the sovereignty of Serbia. It created a flag following a competition, and three projects were chosen by a group of experts and politicians. The final choice was made by their parliament. The chosen design reflected Kosovo's desire to be part of Europe and bears a blue background, like the flag of Bosnia and Herzegovina. The two flags also feature white stars: On Kosovo's flag, the stars represent the different ethnic communities that make up the country, while on Bosnia and Herzegovina's flag, they evoke the European Union.

1

Autonomous Province

In addition to the entities on the opposite page, the former Yugoslavia also housed an autonomous province, Vojvodina, located in northern Serbia.

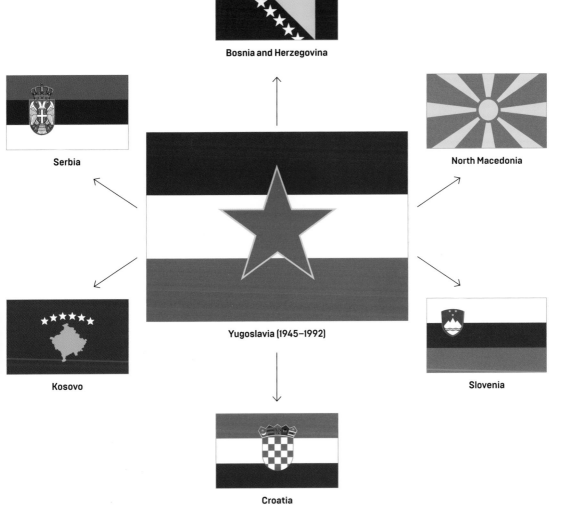

Bosnia and Herzegovina

Serbia

North Macedonia

Yugoslavia (1945–1992)

Kosovo

Slovenia

Croatia

Independence

In 1992, four of the republics that made up Yugoslavia gained their independence. From 1945 to 1991, Kosovo was an autonomous province connected to Serbia within Yugoslavia; today, its sovereignty is disputed.

CHAPTER 4

A HISTORY OF NATIONS

A flag embodies not only the history of a country but also its people. It reflects their hopes, glorifies their past, recalls their battles and victories, honors their heritage and symbolizes a need for renewal. Whether a flag is associated with a nation, state, province, region, canton or city, it is a source of pride for its citizens and plays a unifying role in a place's political, cultural and social life.

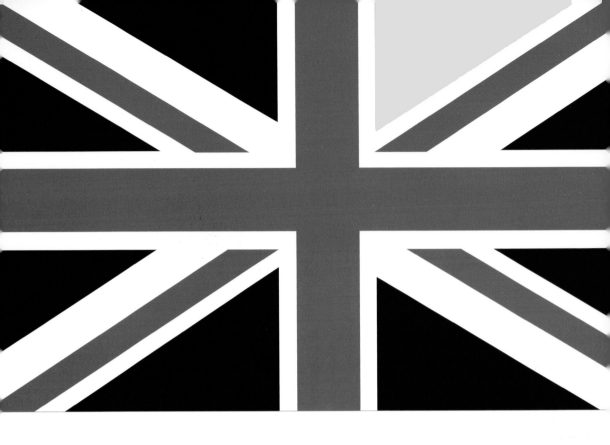

THE UNITED KINGDOM

The origin of the Union Jack reflects the history of the union of the four regions that today make up the United Kingdom.

Nicknamed the Union Jack or the Union Flag, the flag of the United Kingdom was born in 1606 to celebrate the union of the English and Scottish crowns, when King James VI of Scotland became King James I of Great Britain. The blue, white and red flag, which combines both the English and Scottish flags, was not officially used until after the 1707 Act of Union. Wales, which was already integrated in the Kingdom of England, is not represented on the flag. In 1801, following the Act of Union that unified the kingdoms of Great Britain and Ireland, the flag was modified to integrate the Saint Patrick's Cross, the symbol of Ireland.

3
Overlapping Flags

The Union Jack superimposes the English, Scottish and Irish flags. The Saint Andrew's Cross is white and provides the blue background, and both the Saint George's Cross and Saint Patrick's Cross are red (the latter, like the Saint Andrew's Cross, has an X shape).

The Commonwealth of Nations

16

parliamentary monarchies

have the Queen of England as their sovereign.

54

countries

are Commonwealth members in 2020.

Founded in 1949, as the British Empire began to decolonize, the Commonwealth of Nations is a multilateral intergovernmental organization that comprises 54 member states, mostly former territories of the British Empire. Elizabeth II is the head and reigns over 16 parliamentary monarchies throughout the world, all of which are affiliated with the Commonwealth. All members are free, equal and sovereign countries and committed to the Commonwealth Charter for democracy, human rights, non-discrimination, freedom of expression and separation of powers. These states are partners; their only obligations toward one another are to help the most vulnerable, support each other's development and defend each other. To join, it is necessary to have a link to the United Kingdom or a member state, although Mozambique and Rwanda are exceptions to that rule. And it couldn't be simpler to leave! That is what the Maldives, Ireland and Zimbabwe did. Zimbabwe was suspended from the Commonwealth after the election of Robert Mugabe in 2002 and left the organization the following year. Today, the country is negotiating its return. The Maldives rejoined the Commonwealth in 2020. The Commonwealth represents 2.4 billion inhabitants, about one-third of the world's population, of which 60% are younger than 30 years old and 1.3 billion live in India. The Commonwealth has its own flag consisting of the organization's symbol, a radial grid in the shape of a C surrounding a line-covered globe.

In 1982, Queen Elizabeth II, head of the Commonwealth of Nations, made an official visit to Tuvalu (Polynesia).

A procession of flags of member nations at the closing ceremony of the 1958 Commonwealth Games, a multisport competition among the best athletes in the Commonwealth community. That year's event was held at Cardiff Arms Park.

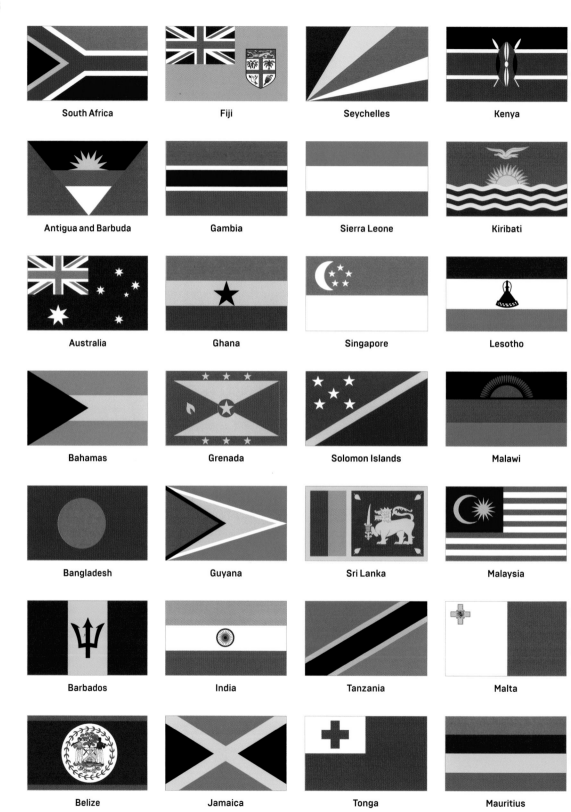

South Africa

Fiji

Seychelles

Kenya

Antigua and Barbuda

Gambia

Sierra Leone

Kiribati

Australia

Ghana

Singapore

Lesotho

Bahamas

Grenada

Solomon Islands

Malawi

Bangladesh

Guyana

Sri Lanka

Malaysia

Barbados

India

Tanzania

Malta

Belize

Jamaica

Tonga

Mauritius

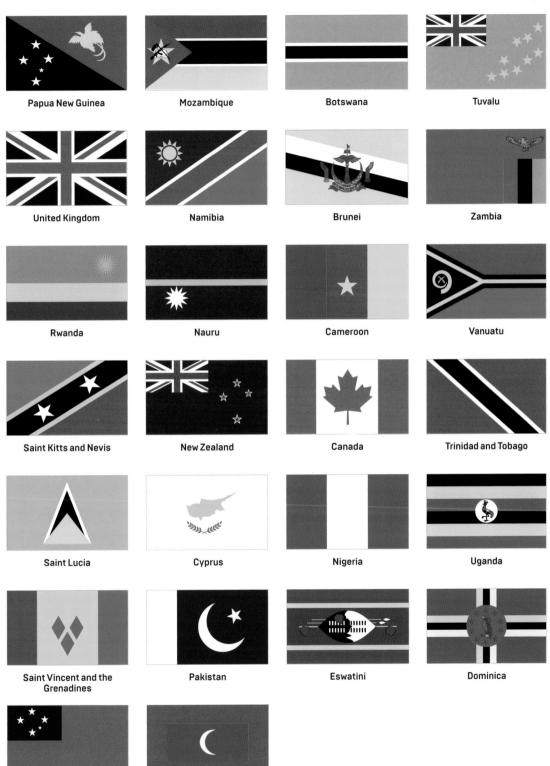

Papua New Guinea

Mozambique

Botswana

Tuvalu

United Kingdom

Namibia

Brunei

Zambia

Rwanda

Nauru

Cameroon

Vanuatu

Saint Kitts and Nevis

New Zealand

Canada

Trinidad and Tobago

Saint Lucia

Cyprus

Nigeria

Uganda

Saint Vincent and the Grenadines

Pakistan

Eswatini

Dominica

Samoa

Maldives

FRANCE

Before the tricolor flag, the Kingdom of France had several standards but no official flag. Among the emblems of France's Ancien Régime was the royal banner with gold fleurs-de-lis on a blue background, which accompanied the king on the battlefield.

Under the reign of Charles V (1364-1380), five rows of fleurs-de-lis were reduced to three flowers to symbolize the Holy Trinity. The origins of the fleur-de-lis are uncertain. They may be the stylized version of the Franks' iron spear, shaped like a harpoon or, according to legend, the flowers are the yellow irises chosen by Clovis to replace the three toads on his coat of arms after the victory at Vouillé in 507. Another symbol of the French monarchy, the use of the color white dates back to the time of the Crusades.

Between 1147 (the second Crusade) and 1418 (the Armagnac-Burgundian Civil War), French kings occasionally (though rarely) also used the oriflamme of the Abbey of Saint Denis as a standard.

On July 14, 1789, the Parisians who stormed the Bastille donned rosettes with the colors of Paris: blue and red. General Lafayette, a hero of the American Revolution, added the color white. He had the National Guard wear tricolor rosettes and offered one to Louis XVI as a sign of reconciliation. In 1790, there was still no official national flag, but the first attempts used those three colors, arranged in horizontal stripes: the white, red and blue of the Fête de la Fédération (July 14, 1790) became red, white and blue upon Louis XVI's execution (January 21, 1793), and finally blue, white and red for the Festival of the Supreme Being in June 1794. In 1790, the Constituent Assembly had imposed on French ships a white ensign with a canton of red, white and blue stripes. In 1794, the new naval ensign with vertical blue, white and red stripes, designed by painter Jacques-Louis David, became the national flag.

1830

The tricolor flag of the French Republic has not been changed since 1830, and it was incorporated in the Constitution of the Fifth Republic in 1958.

As Seen on TV

There is a "television version" of the flag used during presidential addresses. It has a smaller white stripe, so that during close-ups more than just the white section is on screen. In addition, the blue is lighter and the red is brighter.

French Regions and Departments

France's territorial and administrative divisions are referred to as departments or regions. Departments were established in 1789, when provinces had limited powers. In 1946, departments became true territorial collectivities governed by elected councils. Regions were founded between 1954 and 1963, in a bid to limit the degree of administrative centralization in France. Regions comprise several departments without always following the borders of former provinces. The flags of departments and regions were often created based on the coats of arms of French departments designed by heraldist Robert Louis in 1950. Today, department flags are rarely flown, leaving room for the flags of the region and Europe. By 2015, the number of regions had gone from 27 to 18 (13 metropolitan regions and 5 overseas). Over time, new flags had been needed. Some combined regional blazons, such as the flags of Auvergne-Rhône-Alps, Burgundy-Franche-Comté, Pays de la Loire and Provence-Alps-Côte d'Azur. Others were simplified with a common symbol, like the flags of Nouvelle-Aquitaine and Occitanie. Brittany and Corsica retained their flags — the former with its black and white stripes and ermine tips on the canton, the latter with a Moor's head, which the region adopted as its emblem in 1755. Brittany and Corsica are among the few regions to have formalized their regional flag and fly it regularly. There are very few other regional councils that gave their flags official status, most preferring to use their modern and stylized logo, which is easily identifiable.

Île-de-France

Few inhabitants of Île-de-France recognize the non-official regional flag, which has three fleurs-de-lis on a blue background, evocative of the former domain of the kings of France. The flag flown at schools managed by the region has an eight-point star (for the eight regional departments).

Burgundy-Franche-Comté

Auvergne-Rhône-Alps

Provence-Alps-Côte d'Azur

Normandy

Occitanie

Nouvelle-Aquitaine

Corsica

Grand Est

Brittany

Pays de la Loire

Hauts-de-France

French Guiana

Guadeloupe

Martinique

Mayotte

Réunion

Centre-Val de Loire

Auvergne-Rhône-Alps

Auvergne

Lyonnais

Dauphiné

Savoie

New Regions, Ancient History

In the past, metropolitan France was made up of 38 provinces, all possessing a flag and coat of arms. Some present-day regions simply tailored their flag to reflect the union the new territory symbolizes, combining the former flags of its constituent regions, such as the flag of Auvergne-Rhône-Alps (see above).

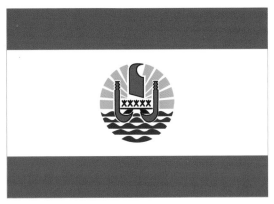

French Polynesia

New Caledonia

Saint Barthélemy

Saint Martin

France's Overseas Regions

France comprises a total of 12 overseas territories. Five of these territories are regions (at left), and seven are collectivities with specific institutions and statuses. In total, these territories are home to 2.6 million inhabitants — that's 4% of the French population.

French Southern and Antarctic Lands

Wallis and Futuna

Saint Pierre and Miquelon

SPAIN

Spain's flag is a combination of elements: blood red and gold colors together with a coat of arms that integrates the emblems of the ancient Kingdoms of Aragon, Castile, León and Navarre. At the bottom of the shield sits a pomegranate, which is the symbol of Granada.

On either side of the coat of arms, the two Pillars of Hercules represent the Canary and Balearic Islands. Adopted in 1785 by the navy to replace the white ensign of the Bourbons, this naval ensign became the emblem of the Spanish army in 1843, and it was then adopted as the national flag in 1874 by King Alfonso XIII. In 1931, the Second Spanish Republic chose a tricolor flag with purple, which would remain the flag of Spanish Republic supporters during the civil war. The government of this republic, in exile in Mexico and then France, kept the flag until 1977. At the same time, in Spain, the nationalists readopted the red and yellow flag. The Franco regime added the coats of arms of Catholic kings and the eagle of Saint John. With the return of the monarchy, the eagle took flight and disappeared from the flag.

3165
square feet

(294 m²) is the surface area of the world's biggest Spanish flag , which is about 69 feet long by 46 feet wide (21 m x 14 m). It is raised once a month above Madrid's Plaza de Colón. In 2017, a businessman from Madrid beat this record by displaying a flag that was more than 7,858 square feet (730 m²) across a 12-story building under construction.

1874–1931
Bourbon Restoration

This flag, a naval emblem in use since 1745, was chosen as the national flag by Alfonso XIII in 1874.

1931–1939
Second Republic

The purple was an homage to the banner of the towns in Castile that led an armed revolt against the absolutist power of Charles I of Spain (Charles V, Holy Roman Emperor) in 1520 and 1521.

1945–1977
Francoist Spain

The eagle of Saint John is on the flag adopted in 1945, which would become the emblem of the Francoist regime.

1981
Kingdom of Spain

The national coats of arms of the six original kingdoms can be seen in this composite blazon. The motto *Plus ultra* ("further beyond") was the motto of the former colonial Spanish Empire, located largely across the Atlantic.

17
flags

28
castles and
towers

20
crowns (11 of
which are on
lions)

19
crosses

14
lions

2
dogs

1
dragon

Autonomous Communities of Spain

Since 1983, Spain has been divided into 17 autonomous communities that consolidate the former kingdoms and provinces of Spain. The flag of Andalusia refers to ancient history, with Hercules dominating over the lions, and tells the story of the Moorish era of Al-Andalus, which began in the 8th century. Other flags evoke victories of Christian leaders (Asturias, Aragon). The flag of Asturias thus bears the emblem of King Pelagius the Conqueror, who initiated the Reconquista in the 8th century. The 28 fortified castles and numerous crosses seen on the coats of arms of autonomous Spanish regions reflect the Reconquista, during which Christian troops fought the Moors for 700 years, until the fall of Granada in 1492.

Andalusia

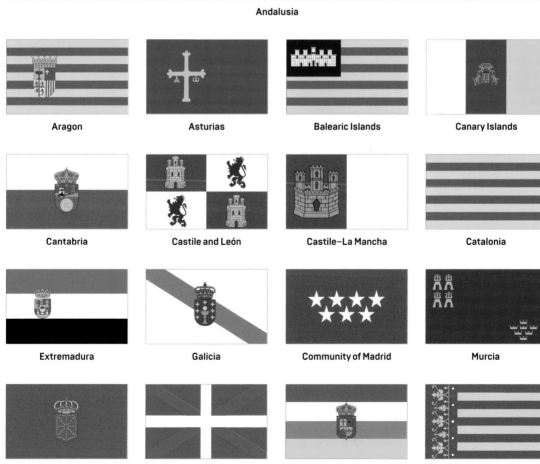

Aragon	Asturias	Balearic Islands	Canary Islands

Cantabria	Castile and León	Castile–La Mancha	Catalonia

Extremadura	Galicia	Community of Madrid	Murcia

Navarre	Basque Country	La Rioja	Valencian Community

ITALY

2006
is the year
when a law
established
the current colors of
the Italian flag, which
are Pantone Matching
System shades called
Fern Green, Bright
White and Flame
Scarlet.

Before becoming unified in 1848, Italy had long been a mosaic of small independent states (republics, duchies, kingdoms, principalities), each with its own flag.

It was only in 1797, after Napoleon's victory in the Italian campaign, that the first flags with three stripes of green, white and red appeared, taking after the French tricolor flag. The Transpadane Republic had a flag with three vertical stripes of green, white and red, and the Cispadane Republic had a flag with horizontal stripes of the same colors. The Cisalpine Republic (1797–1802) adopted both versions. At the end of the 19th century, the French flag also had horizontal stripes.

It is said that Napoleon preferred green over blue, so he chose these colors for the uniforms for the army of Lombardy. One can also see an allusion to Dante in the flag. In his 18th-century chant Purpatorie, Beatrice, his muse, is associated with three colors, and each color is tied to a theological virtue: green for hope, white for faith and red for charity. Some prefer to discern the colors of the hills of the Apennine Mountains, the snow of the Alps and the blood of the martyrs of the 19th-century Wars of Independence. Foodies almost certainly see the flag in their margherita pizza — the basil, mozzarella and tomatoes replicate Italy's national colors!

It is said that Napoleon preferred green over blue, so he chose these colors for the uniforms of the army of Lombardy.

An illustration of the Italian delegation during a republican procession in 1797 in France, during the time of the French Directory.

Italian Regions

There is little unity among the flags of the 20 Italian regions. Some flags depict postcard-worthy landscapes — like the mountains (white), natural parks (green) and Adriatic Sea (blue) that contribute to the richness of Abruzzo, or the four rivers, represented by four stylized waves, that flow through Basilicata. Others provide snapshots of Italy's history from antiquity to the Renaissance, such as the Camunian rose (*rosa camuna*), a cross with rounded shapes copied from a Val Camonica rock carving, which appears on the flag of Lombardy; the woodpecker on the flag of Marche, which is a symbol of the ancient people of Picenum (Picenes), who unified the region in the Iron Age; and the gorgon and triskelion (a being with three legs in a spiral)on Sicily's flag, which refer to the region's Minoan origins. There is also the winged lion of Venice that sits proudly on the flag of Veneto and Tuscany's rearing pegasus, sculpted by Cellini, at the center of its flag. The four Moorish heads on the Sardinian flag evoke the fight against the Muslims, when the island belonged to the Kingdom of Aragon. A few flags were derived from heraldry: Aosta Valley and Molise reincorporated the coats of arms of noble families, and Latium combined the coats of arms from its five provinces, which created a flag full of information.

The Moors

The four Moorish heads on the Sardinian flag evoke the fight against the Muslims, when the island belonged to the Kingdom of Aragon.

Tuscany

20
Italian regions

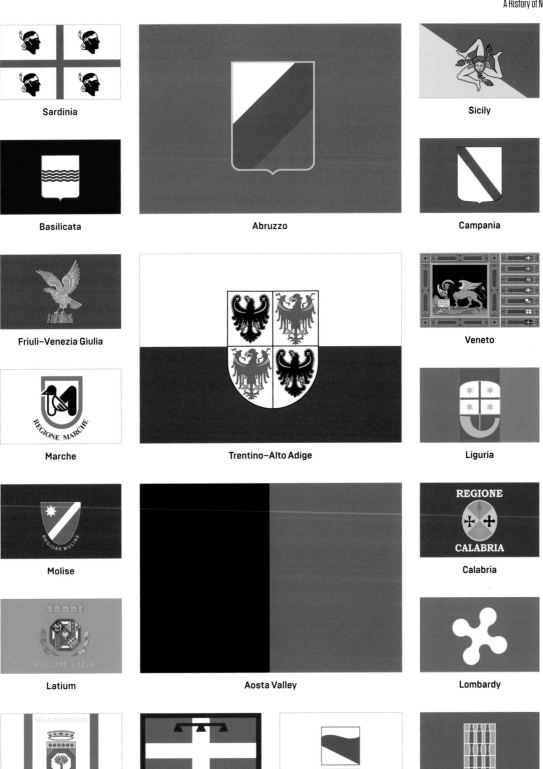

Sardinia

Basilicata

Abruzzo

Sicily

Campania

Friuli–Venezia Giulia

Marche

Trentino–Alto Adige

Veneto

Liguria

Molise

Aosta Valley

Calabria

Latium

Lombardy

Puglia

Piedmont

Emilia-Romagna

Umbria

JAPAN

Hi no maru no hata, the "circle of the sun flag," was formally recognized in the 20th century and bears a centuries-old motif among the people of Japan.

The Japanese flag, a crimson red circle representing the sun on a white background, symbolizes purity, honesty and passion. The sun disk is an ancient motif that was used in 701 on Emperor Monmu's standard and has been frequently used since, particularly on the banners of samurai and shogun. It conjures up images of Japan as the "origin of the sun" that rises in the east — hence Japan's nickname, "Land of the Rising Sun." According to legend, the 13th-century Buddhist monk Nichiren offered a standard bearing the sun disk to the emperor, who was considered a descendent of the Shinto sun goddess Amaterasu. This divine symbol protected the empire against the Mongols. The sun disk brought luck to the Japanese who fought off the Mongol invasion lead by Genghis Khan. In 1868, with the Meiji Restoration and the return of imperial power, the bright-red sun disk became one of the empire's symbols, along with the famous rising sun surrounded by rays that adorns the ensign of the Japanese Navy. The national flag was not made official until 1999. It was named *Nisshoki* ("flag of Japan") in official documents and *Hi no maru* (sun disk) by the public, who sometimes offer it as a lucky charm by writing messages of good luck or encouragement in the form of rays around the sun disk.

1999
Official recognition of the Japanese flag with the sun disk.

The sun disk originally symbolized a 13th-century Japanese emperor who, according to legend, was a descendant of the sun goddess Amaterasu (opposite).

Japanese Prefectures

Japan in divided into eight regions and 47 prefectures that are territorial or administrative divisions created in 1871 by the Meiji government and permanently established in 1888. Numbered from 1 to 47 from north to south, they do not correspond to former fiefs nor historical provinces, but rather to a division of the country into rural departments based on economic equality. Despite the country's high degree of urbanization, the prefectures have remained unchanged. All but four have the same status: the metropolitan prefecture of Tokyo, the island prefecture of Hokkaido, and the prefectures of Osaka and Kyoto, which lost their distinction in 1947, with the Local Autonomy Law. Each prefecture has its own flag designed according to a simple and identical scheme: a solid background with a symbol or kanji at its center. Most of these flags use only two or three colors, but each color holds a specific meaning. For example, green is for the abundance of nature and hope; white for snow, purity and infinity; red for progress and passion; blue for the sky, sea and harmony; orange for friendship and unity; and yellow for the sun or rapeseed flowers. The highly stylized motif in the center is often the emblem of the prefecture, which can be a katakana, kanji or hiragana (the three characters used in Japanese writing) or a symbol tied to the natural or economic resources of the prefecture — mountain, river, sea, rosebud, sun, bird, harbor, etc. — often in a poetic or pictorial form.

Todofuken

Today, all the prefectures are referred to as *todofuken*, a word derived from the kanji (Chinese characters used in Japanese writing) for the four former types of prefectures (*to, dō, fu, ken*).

Niigata Prefecture

Hiroshima Prefecture

Toyama Prefecture

Fukui Prefecture

Nagano Prefecture

Kanagawa Prefecture

Saitama Prefecture

Nara Prefecture

Aomori Prefecture

Miyagi Prefecture

Aichi Prefecture

Kochi Prefecture

Akita Prefecture

Fukushima Prefecture

Oita Prefecture

Kagoshima Prefecture

Okinawa Prefecture

Gifu Prefecture

Kumamoto Prefecture

Miyazaki Prefecture

Shimane Prefecture

Yamaguchi Prefecture

A Beautiful Bouquet

The flowers found on the flags of five Japanese prefectures (Ibaraki: the rose; Kyoto: the cherry blossom; Ehime: the mandarin blossom; Fukuoka: the plum blossom; and Saga: the camphor blossom) are either the symbol of the prefecture or an emblem that represents the region's harmonious development.

Kyoto Prefecture

Fukuoka Prefecture

Saga Prefecture

Hokkaido Prefecture

Ehime Prefecture

Ibaraki Prefecture

Wakayama Prefecture

Yamanashi Prefecture

Tochigi Prefecture

Ishikawa Prefecture

Gunma Prefecture

Tokyo Metropolis

Chiba Prefecture

Iwate Prefecture

Yamagata Prefecture

Tokushima Prefecture

Shizuoka Prefecture

Hyogo Prefecture

Shiga Prefecture

Kagawa Prefecture

Mie Prefecture

Osaka Prefecture

Tottori Prefecture

Nagasaki Prefecture

Okayama Prefecture

PEOPLE'S REPUBLIC OF CHINA

The red flag with one large star and four smaller ones commemorates the revolution and unity of the four social classes of Chinese people under the authority of the Communist Party.

Created following a contest, this design by Zeng Liansong was chosen among entries from 38 finalists. Attracted by the ideals of revolution, he worked on it at night, which is how the idea of stars came about. Mao Zedong preferred another design, with a yellow horizontal line representing the Yellow River and a large star in the canton, but the other committee members considered the golden stripe too divisive. It was Zeng's red field that prevailed. The hammer and sickle of the initial design were removed, since these were too reminiscent of the USSR. The first "five-starred red flag" was raised by Mao Zedong above Tiananmen Square on October 1, 1949.

56
Ethnicities

The Chinese population is 92% Han, and the remaining 8% is split between 55 ethnic minorities.

Mao Zedong's first choice

1644–1912
Qing Dynasty

This imperial flag dates back to 1889, during the Qing Dynasty (1644–1912). The dragon transfers its cosmic power to the emperor so that he may reign in harmony with nature.

1912–1928
Republic of China

The five colors represent the five main peoples of China: Han (red), Manchu (yellow), Mongol (blue), Hui (white) and Tibetan (black).

1928–1949
Republic of China

"Blue sky, white sun and a wholly red earth" is the name of this flag, currently the flag of the Republic of China (commonly called Taiwan). The red represents luck and happiness.

1949
People's Republic of China

The five-starred red flag was raised for the first time on October 1, 1949, with the founding of the People's Republic of China.

The Chinese Provinces

According to the 1982 Constitution, the People's Republic of China is officially divided into 23 provinces (including the Republic of China, better known as Taiwan, which is claimed as the 23rd province), four municipalities (Beijing, Shanghai, Tianjin and Chongqing), five autonomous regions (Inner Mongolia, Guangxi, Tibet, Ningxia and Xinjiang) and two special administrative regions (Hong Kong and Macao). The provinces and autonomous regions are themselves divided into departments, districts and municipalities and then into townships and villages.

The provinces and municipalities report directly to the central authority, while autonomous regions are territories managed autonomously by the ethnic minorities, at least partially. Hong Kong and Macao are exceptions and subject to fundamental laws passed by the National People's Congress. In these two special administrative regions, the "one country, two systems" principle governs political and economic life. This provides significant autonomy to the local government, with the exception of decisions regarding foreign affairs and defense, which remain in the hands of the Chinese government.

34 Administrative Regions: 3 Flags

By order of the government, cities and provinces are not permitted to have their own flag. The only two exceptions are Macao and Hong Kong, which have very significant autonomy relative to the Chinese government. This system is guaranteed until 2047 for Hong Kong and 2049 for Macao.

Hong Kong

Macao

THE UNITED STATES OF AMERICA

With 32 variations, it is the flag that has undergone the most changes over the course of its history.

When the flag was created in 1777, it had 13 horizontal stripes, representing the 13 Confederate States, founders of the American nation: Connecticut, New Hampshire, New York, New Jersey, Massachusetts, Pennsylvania, Delaware, Virginia, North Carolina, South Carolina, Georgia, Rhode Island and Maryland. Traditionally, the stripes are sewn together to symbolize the union between the states. In the upper left corner of the original flag, a blue rectangle featured 13 white stars for the 13 original states. At the time, there was no specific rule, and the stars were arranged sometimes in a circle, sometimes in a line. There were up to 27 different American flags in use at the same time!

13
stripes:
7 red
and **6** white

50
white stars
with **5** points

Interior of an American
post office, 1925.

> ## "We take the stars from heaven, the red from our mother country, separating it by white stripes, thus showing that we have separated from her."
>
> George Washington

In 1795, after Vermont and Kentucky joi-
ned the Confederacy, the flag changed and
had 15 stars and 15 red and white stripes.
However, after five new states entered the
Confederacy, the flag reverted to 13 stripes and only the
number of stars increased. In 1912, then-president William
Howard Taft ordered that the flag have five-pointed stars
near the top arranged in nine rows of five and six stars. In
1959, the banner's proportions were definitively set. Today,
the use of the flag, nicknamed the Stars and Stripes and
Old Glory, is governed by strict protocol, called the Flag
Code. The next two stars could represent the District of
Columbia and the territory of Puerto Rico, which hope to
become full-fledged states.

On Inauguration Day 2017,
five flags (two duplicates)
were hung on the facade of
the United States Capitol.
In addition to the current
national flag (center)
and the Betsy Ross flag
(far right and far left),
two flags with 13 stars
were displayed in honor
of Donald Trump's home
state, New York, which is
one of the original states.

The States

Each U.S. state and territory (entities that are independent of the 50 states) has a flag. A total of 33 flags feature the state's name, seal or motto on a solid, often blue, background. These include the flags of the 13 original states, which came together in 1776. Many flags also evoke the region's natural resources and its history, such as the palm tree for South Carolina and the copper star for Arizona. Sometimes virtues are symbolized; for example, strength is illustrated by the Ursa Major (or Big Dipper) constellation on the Alaskan flag, designed in 1927 by 13-year-old Benny Benson, and the California grizzly bear on the Californian flag. The bear that served as the model was the last of this subspecies, which is now extinct. Nicknamed "Bear Flag," the Californian flag was adopted in 1911. Most states created their flags around the turn of the 20th century, particularly during the world's fairs in Chicago (1893), St. Louis (1904) and San Francisco (1915). All these flags are rectangular in shape, except for Ohio's, adopted in 1902, which is pentagonal. Most of these flags have been modified over their history, and some have been modified several times. Most recently, the flag of the Commonwealth of the Northern Mariana Islands was changed in 1985 and the Utah state flag in 2011. The newest flag is Hawaii's, which was adopted in 1959.: Created in 1843, it combines the American and British flags. It was successively the flag of the Republic of Hawaii (1843–1893), the territory of Hawaii (1894–1959) and the state of Hawaii (since 1959). Its eight white, red and blue horizontal stripes represent its eight major islands, and the Union Jack in the canton recalls when Hawaii was under British rule.

50
state flags

33
feature the state seal or coat of arms

31
display a motto

27
bear the state name or its initials

25
have a blue background

14
display a date

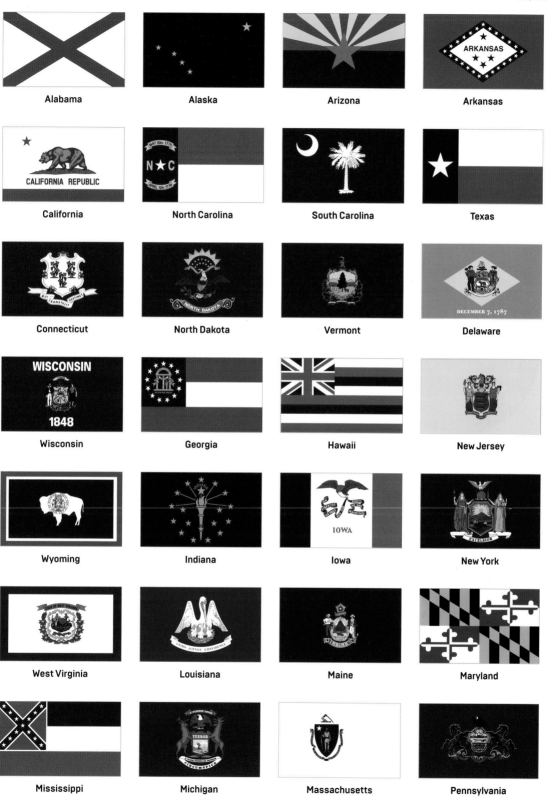

Alabama

Alaska

Arizona

Arkansas

California

North Carolina

South Carolina

Texas

Connecticut

North Dakota

Vermont

Delaware

Wisconsin

Georgia

Hawaii

New Jersey

Wyoming

Indiana

Iowa

New York

West Virginia

Louisiana

Maine

Maryland

Mississippi

Michigan

Massachusetts

Pennsylvania

The Seal: A Historic Emblem

A seal is the equivalent of a coat of arms or blazon. The Great Seal of
the United States is the federal emblem, and there's even one for the
president. Each state also has their own seal; 33 out of 50 states (66%)
feature it on their flag.

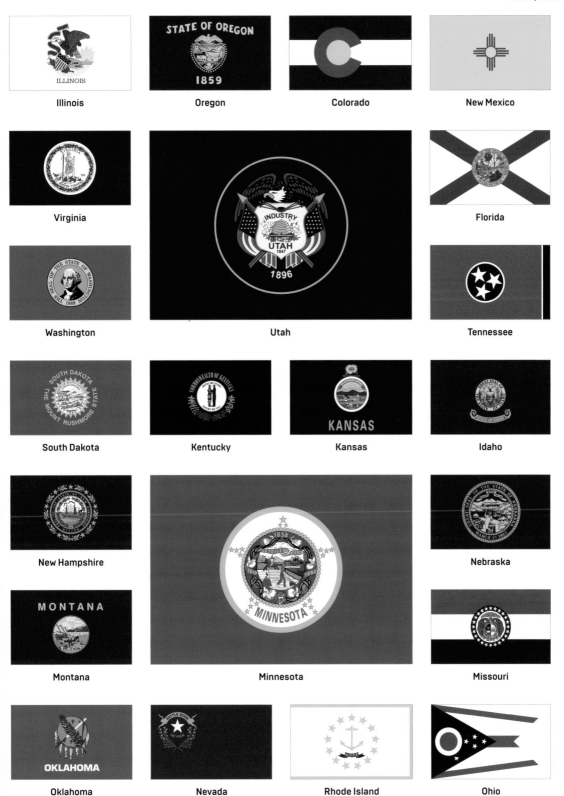

Illinois

Oregon

Colorado

New Mexico

Virginia

Florida

Washington

Utah

Tennessee

South Dakota

Kentucky

Kansas

Idaho

New Hampshire

Nebraska

Montana

Minnesota

Missouri

Oklahoma

Nevada

Rhode Island

Ohio

GERMANY

Since reunification, Germany's flag has remained black, red and gold, but its history goes back to the 13th century.

In the 13th century, the imperial banner of the Holy Roman Empire featured a black eagle on a gold background, which became a double-headed eagle in the 15th century. In 1806, the Confederation of the Rhine, established by Napoleon Bonaparte, used both a flag with horizontal green, white and blue stripes and the French tricolor flag. In 1815, the German Confederation founded by the Congress of Vienna chose a black, red and yellow flag. In 1867, Bismarck formed the North German Confederation, whose flag combined the colors of Prussia and the Hanseatic League. It was also the flag of the German Empire (1871 -1918), which was then replaced with the Nazi flag by the Third Reich in 1933. In 1935, Hitler made the swastika the national flag. In 1949, the German Federal Republic and the German Democratic Republic used the same black, red and yellow flag. In 1959, East Germany added their coats of arms to celebrate the union of the classes.

8
Times per Year

According to a 2005 federal decree, the flag must fly above public buildings during eight special days (not necessarily public holidays), including the anniversary of the liberation of Auschwitz, the anniversary of German reunification and Labor Day.

15th C.
Holy Empire

The Holy Roman Empire, called the Holy Roman Empire of the German Nation in the 15th century, lasted more than 800 years. The flag with a double-headed eagle is the imperial banner used between the 10th and 15th centuries and again in the 19th century.

1815
German Confederation

The flag bears the colors of the current national flag but with a different proportion (3:2). They are the colors of the Urburschenschaft student association, established in 1815 at the University of Jena, which campaigned for the unification of Germany.

1871
German Empire

This flag combines the colors of Prussia (black and white) and the Hanseatic League (red and white).

1933
The Third Reich

Adolf Hitler thrust Germany into the Second World War, and the flag — with white for nationalism, red for socialism and the swastika for the Aryan race — was displayed in every European country under Nazi occupation.

1949
East Germany

After the war, Germany was divided in two: the German Federal Republic (West) and the German Democratic Republic (East). The black, red and gold flag of Eastern Germany featured a blazon with communist emblems tied to the USSR.

1990
Reunification

The Germanies came together under the same flag, the one adopted by West Germany in 1949.

Die Fahnen

LUBECK

HESS CASSEL

BREMEN

HESS DARMSTADT

NASSAU

BAVARIA

NORTH GERMANY

BADEN

GERMANY

Publ. by Wm. C. Robertson, 59 Cedar St. N.Y.

THE FLAGS OF

1871

The German Empire was founded

following the defeat
of Napoleon III of
France during the
Franco-Prussian War.
William I of Prussia
(top row, center),
was then proclaimed
kaiser (emperor). It
was the culmination
of unification efforts
between various cities
and regions (see flags
opposite) initiated by
Bismarck (bottom row,
right) in the 1860s.

Brandenburg

German Länder

Germany is composed of federal states, called LänderSince 1990 there are 16 such states. Each has a constitution, a government (or senate) and an assembly elected by universal ballot. The states are sovereign and have a high degree of authority, particularly regarding education, police, cultural affairs and local government. That explains why their flags are so prevalent in civil and political life and why the people are so attached to them. Although these states all have the same legal status in Germany, they do not all have the same title: Some have retained a name inherited from the past, particularly from the Holy Roman Empire. For example, there are *Freistaat* (a free state or "republic"), like Bavaria, Saxony and Thuringia, and there are city-states, like Berlin (the capital) as well as Bremen and Hamburg, which are two equally "free and Hanseatic" cities.

2
Hanseatic City-States
Bremen and Hamburg were once part of the Hanseatic League, the powerful league of merchant cities along the North and Baltic Seas, which played a major role in business and politics in Northern Europe between the 12th and 17th centuries.

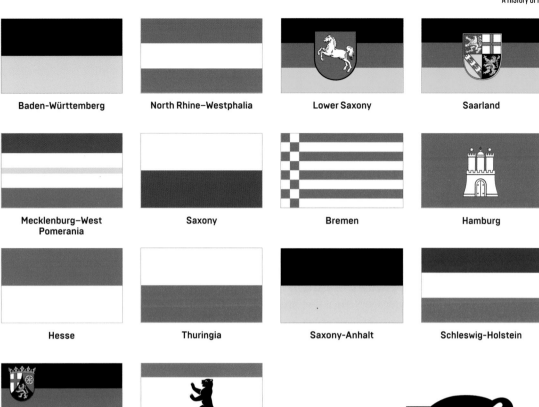

Baden-Württemberg	North Rhine–Westphalia	Lower Saxony	Saarland
Mecklenburg–West Pomerania	Saxony	Bremen	Hamburg
Hesse	Thuringia	Saxony-Anhalt	Schleswig-Holstein

 Rhineland-Palatinate

 Berlin

Bavaria

Ancient Inspiration

All of the flags of German *Länder* are inspired by the colors and coats of arms on the blazons of former cities and regions. For example, Berlin's emblem is the famous bear standing on its hind legs, nicknamed *Berliner Bär* ("Berlin Bear"), which was used on the city's seal as early as 1280. The bear symbolizes the inhabitants of Berlin; however, for centuries, it had a collar and was held on a leash by an eagle, alluding to the submission of the people of Berlin to the authority of the House of Hohenzollern. The leash and collar disappeared in 1920, and the bear has straightened up to become this proud and daring animal.

SWITZERLAND

The Swiss federal flag, with a white cross on a red background, was created in 1840 and enshrined in the Constitution in 1848. Its square shape symbolizes equality between the north, south, east and west.

The flags of Switzerland and Vatican City are the only square flags. The origin of the Swiss flag's red background remains a subject of debate among historians. For some, it is reminiscent of the Bernese flag, while for others it evokes the blood of Christ or the blood shed for the country. The white cross in the middle marks the separation of powers between the confederation (cantons and communes) and the executive, legislative and judicial powers. The arms of the cross are one-sixth longer than they are wide. The origin of this flag dates to 1339, when Swiss soldiers sewed a white cross on their clothing during the Battle of Laupen, between Bern and Louis IV of Bavaria and his allies. These rallying signs helped the Swiss solders distinguish themselves from their enemies. Very quickly, this cross appeared on all of the Swiss troops' the banners. When Napoleon Bonaparte founded the Helvetic Republic (1798–1803), he imposed a national tricolor flag of green, red and yellow, which was abandoned just after the fall of the republic.

2
Square Flags
There are only two square flags in the world: the flag of Switzerland and the flag of Vatican City.

Bern

The Swiss Cantons

The Swiss Confederation retained its name, although it is now a federation. Switzerland is made up of 26 federal states, called "cantons," and each has its own constitution, parliament, government and tribunal. The cantons where German is spoken are mostly referred to as states (*Staaten*). However, the cantons of Geneva, Jura, Neuchâtel and Ticino are considered to be both republics and cantons , since they are called "republics" in both French and Italian. Valais and Vaud are republics. Each canton is represented at the National Council, based on its population. They all have square flags with simple and legible motifs inspired by their coats of arms on, mostly, a solid or divided background. They include noble animals and several religious symbols.

The Bear: A Local Legend

One day, Saint Gall, who lived in a cabin in the woods, encountered an aggressive bear. He asked the bear to go fetch him some wood. The bear left in search of wood, and the abbot gave it food in appreciation. He then ordered the bear to leave the country for good, and the bear obeyed. In Switzerland the bear is a symbol of courage, intelligence and vigor.

Thurgau

Uri

Geneva

Graubünden

Basel-Stadt

Vaud

Basel-Land

Appenzell Ausserrhoden

Neuchâtel

Fribourg

Obwalden

Ticino

Zurich

Zug

Solothurn

Lucerne

Appenzell Innerrhoden

Schaffhausen

St. Gallen

Jura

Nidwalden

Glarus

Schwyz

Valais

Aargau

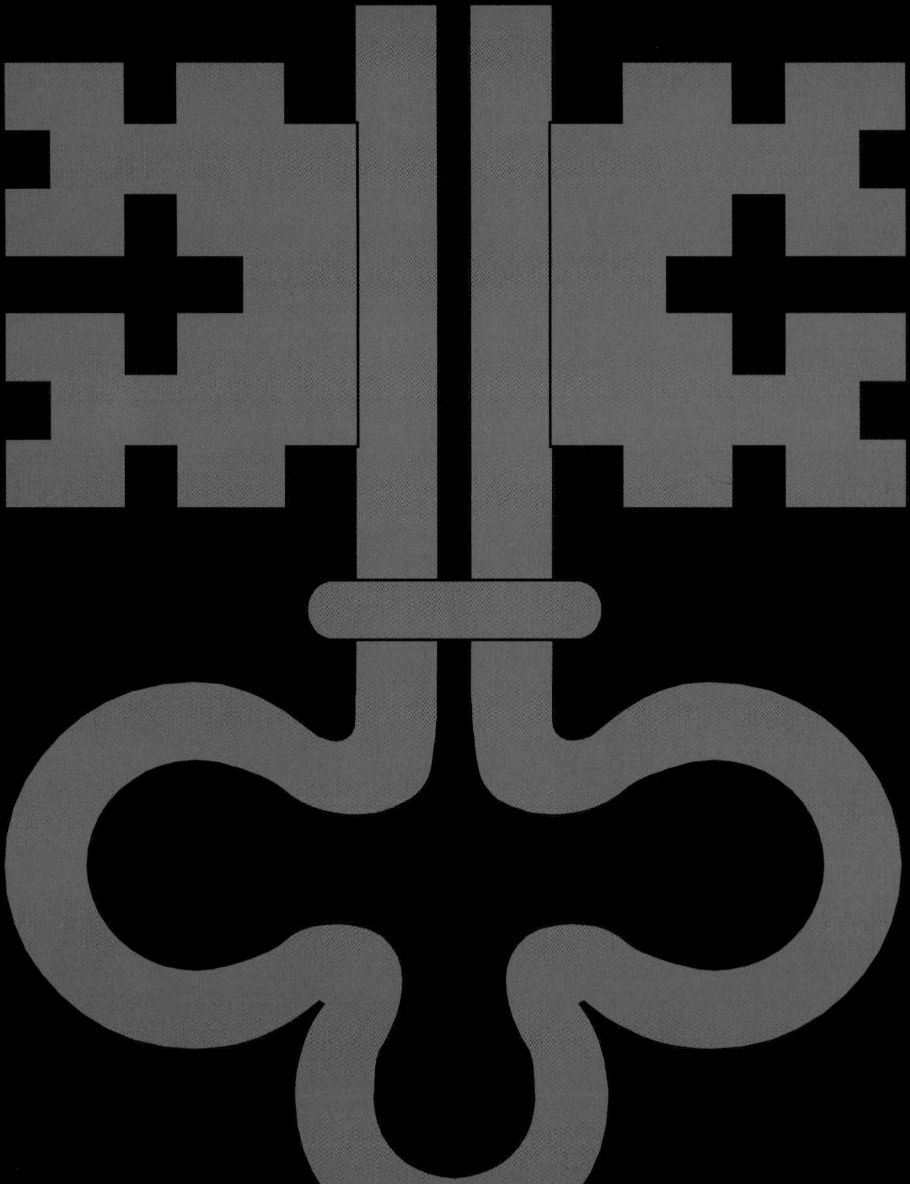

CHAPTER 5

A COMMON IDENTITY

Whether identity is linked to heritage, shared values or a shared culture, countries form unions beyond their national borders. Some are proud to signal their belonging to a continent, their adherence to a doctrine or their attachment to a history, an ethnicity or religious convictions. Whatever the cause or ideal, flags can help express it.

"The Pan-Slavic flag represents faith (blue), peace (white) and revolution (red)."

THE PAN-SLAVIC FLAG

Blue, white and red — those are the colors of the flag of the Russian Empire under the rule of Czar Peter the Great (1682–1725).

Many Slavic countries have flags with blue, white and red. Historically, red was the color of the Byzantine emperor, blue was the color of the Virgin Mary and white was the color of independence. The colors of the Russian flag have other meanings: blue for the bourgeoisie, white for nobility and red for the people. It was Peter the Great who had the idea of associating a color to each class of society. He kept white, which was the emblem of the nobility in France, and chose blue for the bourgeoisie and red for the people. In the 19th century, the Pan-Slavic movement was gaining strength in Europe. This ideology emphasized the common identity of Slavic peoples and advocated for their political union. In 1848, a flag with three horizontal blue, white and red stipes was created for the Prague Slavic Congress. The colors held different meanings from that point on: faith (blue), peace (white) and revolution (red). Blue, white and red had spread over the flags of several European countries by the end of the 19th century, and were then used on the flags of Russia's autonomous republics.

Pan-Slavic flag

83 Subjects

The Russian Federation is made up of 83 entities called "subjects" of the federation, including 21 republics, 9 krais, 46 oblasts, 4 okrugs and 2 federal villages. The flags of certain subjects also bear the Pan-Slavic colors.

Czech Republic

Mordovia

Bosnian Serb Republic

Serbia

Khakassia

Slovenia

Chukotka

Slovakia

Croatia

THE COLORS OF AFRICA

Green, yellow, red: this color combination is found throughout Western African flags and originates with the Ethiopian flag.

Ethiopia is the oldest independent African country. It is also the only one that maintained its sovereignty during the colonizations of the 19th century, after the victory of Emperor Menelik II against the Italians at Adwa in 1896. The flag of the Ethiopian Empire, adopted the following year, has three horizontal stripes of green, yellow and red. The yellow stripe in the center features the Lion of Judah, a symbol of the royal dynasty. The combination of green, yellow and red served as a model for the flags of many other African countries that gained their independence in the 20th century. The first of these was Ghana, in 1957.

Despite several political changes throughout the 20th century, the Ethiopian flag always retained its green, yellow and red horizontal stripes but added different motifs. In 1996, the new flag of the young Federal Democratic Republic of Ethiopia carried on this tradition. Green represents fertile land and hope, yellow represents harmony and justice, and red represents blood and sacrifice. In the center is the symbol of Ethiopia: a blue circle, which symbolizes peace, and a five-point star, which evokes unity among Ethiopian peoples as well as prosperity.

13
African countries
currently have red, yellow and green on their flag.

5
countries outside Africa
have red, yellow and green.

4
countries
with no African heritage have a red, yellow and green flag.

The five-point star evokes unity among Ethiopian peoples as well as prosperity.

Ethiopia

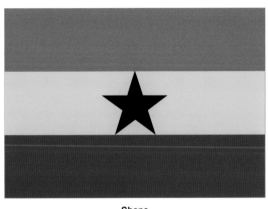

Ghana

Benin

Mali

São Tomé and Príncipe

Togo

Senegal

Guinea-Bissau

Guinea

Mauritania

Republic of the Congo

Cameroon

Burkina Faso

The Pan-African Flag: Red, Black and Green

On the Pan-African flag, the traditional yellow is replaced with black. This flag has been adopted mainly by countries outside of Africa whose population is largely of African origin. The red recalls the blood shed for liberation, black personifies the African people spread across the globe, and green evokes natural resources. Pan-Africanism is a movement of solidarity among African peoples, and they adopted this flag in August 1920, during the Convention of the Universal Negro Improvement Association and African Communities League (UNIA & ACL), which brought together delegates from 25 countries to New York. Article 39 of the Declaration of the Rights of Negro Peoples of the World, drafted at the convention, declares: "That the colors, Red, Black and Green, be the colors of the Negro race."

Pan-African flag

The Pan-African flag displays the African peoples' spirit of self-determination and has become the symbol of African liberation movements around the world. It was born in response to a popular racist song that said: "Every race has a flag but the coon." Those words struck Jamaican Marcus Garvey, a prominent figure in the fight against racial discrimination in the 1920s and founder of the UNIA. This flag remains the expression of the honor and unity of African Peoples, and it is still regularly flown by African nationalists. Many African and Caribbean flags incorporate these three colors as emblems of Pan-Africanism, such as the flags of Malawi and Kenya and Rwanda's first flag (1962–2001).

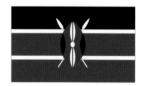

Kenya

Malawi

Marcus Garvey

Marcus Garvey is the
founder of the Universal
Negro Improvement
Association. His
objective was to unite
black people from all
over the world. He lived
most of his life in the
United States.

PAN-ARAB COLORS

The flags of Arab countries are mostly inspired by the flag of the Great Arab Revolt — carried out between 1916 and 1918, to liberate the Arabian Peninsula from the Ottomans — and its colors: black, green, white and red.

This flag was designed by Hussein ben Ali (1853–1931), the Hashemite who was, Sharif of Mecca, led the revolt and became King of Hejaz from 1916 to 1924. The flag of the Great Arab Revolt would become the flag of the Kingdom of Hejaz. There are three horizontal stripes of black, green and white and a red triangle. Each color refers to an Arab dynasty: red for the Hashemites, black for the Abbasids of Baghdad, green for the Fatimids and white for the Umayyads of Damascus. In the Middle Ages, Iraqi poet Safī al-Dīn al-Hilli (1278–1349) celebrated these colors in verse, and they subsequently became symbols of Arab nationalism, promoting the people's common historical, cultural and linguistic heritage. Today, these four colors are combined in different ways on the flags of many Arab countries.

Palestine

9

national flags

currently use the Pan-Arab colors (although Egypt and Yemen omit the green), and several partially recognized states (such as Palestine) and political movements also feature these colors on their flag.

Flag of the Great Arab Revolt

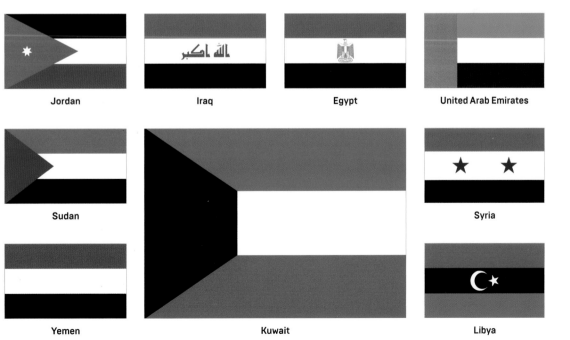

Jordan

Iraq

Egypt

United Arab Emirates

Sudan

Syria

Yemen

Kuwait

Libya

THE EUROPEAN UNION

The European flag is used for both the European Union (27 member states) and the Council of Europe (47 members).

From its inception in 1949, the Council of Europe sought to create a flag that would reflect "the spiritual and moral values which are the common heritage of their peoples." There were then two flags that embodied Europe: the one of the International Paneuropean Union, which was rejected by Turkey, who became the 13th member of the Council of Europe in 1950 — and the one of the European federalists, who were united in the European Movement International and whose flag bears a green E on a white background. The Council of Europe appointed a commission to create a simple, clear and harmonious flag and launched a call for

International Paneuropean Union

Union of European Federalists

Some think the stars of the European flag were borrowed from the first American flag, which was crafted by Betsy Ross (at right), who presented it to George Washington (far left).

The European flag reflects "the spiritual and moral values which are the common heritage of their peoples."

proposals. Out of the hundreds of submissions, a dozen were short-list and the eventual flag of European Communities was adopted in 1955.

It went on to become the flag of the European Union. A symbol of the identity and unity of Europe, the flag bears 12 five-point gold stars (pointing upward) arranged in a circle (like the hours on the face of a clock) on a blue background (for the sky). The stars symbolize unity, solidarity and harmony among the peoples of Europe. The number 12 represents perfection and completeness; it remains fixed no matter the number of member countries. Today, the European flag is a contentious subject due to its possible religious origins. Some see the background color as representative of the Virgin Mary. Others see the 12 stars as a biblical symbol (12 tribes of Israel, 12 apostles or 12 stars on the Virgin Mary's crown). Still others think the stars are borrowed from the first American flag (the Betsy Ross flag, dating from the 18th century), which had a circle of 13 white stars on a blue background in the canton.

THE UN

The United Nations was founded in 1945, at the end of the Second World War, to replace the League of Nations.

Under the guidance of American architect and designer Oliver Lincoln Lundquist, a team of graphic designers created an emblem and a flag to be presented at the San Francisco Conference in August 1945. The result was, in their words, "a map of the world representing an azimuthal equidistant projection centred on the North Pole, inscribed in a wreath consisting of crossed conventionalized branches of the olive tree, in gold on a field of smoke-blue with all water areas in white. The projection of the map extends to 60 degrees south latitude, and includes five concentric circles."

Adopted by the General Assembly on December 7, 1946, this flag uses the two official colors of the United Nations — blue for the background and white for the image. The world map is centered on the North Pole and, thus, does not show Antarctica. However, in 1947, the General Assembly chose a new flag for the UN on which the continents were rotated 90 degrees to the east so that the center of the map lines up with the Greenwich meridian, which is the international reference for longitude. The aim is to ensure perfect neutrality. Some say, however, that it was modified to prevent North America from being in the center of the flag.

"They are also aspirational symbols, for they speak to the hopes and dreams of people the world over, for peace and unity."
Presentation of the UN emblem and flag on the UN website.

The continents are not displayed the same way on the UN's original emblem (see opposite) and its current flag (above). In 1947, the continents were rotated 90 degrees.

ANTARCTICA

Since 1998, Antarctica has been an uninhabited nature reserve devoted to peace, science and environmental protection. It has no official flag, and yet many flags fly on the "white continent."

There are no permanent inhabitants, but about 50 bases are located there, which welcome, depending on the season, between 1,000 and 4,500 scientists who conduct various experiments, primarily on the study of climate. Enforced since 1961, the Antarctic Treaty regulates the relationships between states for any territories south of the 60th parallel, while territories north of the 60th parallel are under the jurisdiction of various sovereign nations. To day, 54 states have signed the Antarctic Treaty. The Antarctic treaty organization does not have an official flag, but it does have a flag that it uses during its annual meetings, which was created in 2002.

There are, however, two official flag projects designed by vexillologists: one flag was designed by Graham Bartram and is very similar to the flag of the Antarctic Treaty, and the other is by Whitney Smith and differs greatly from the current flag, having the letter A on sea ice held in cupped hands, to symbolize peace, on an orange background. Neither of these flags has ever been flown on the territories governed by the treaty.

Many national and regional flags are flown north of the 60th parallel, including those of the British Antarctic Territory, Australia (the Australian Arctic Territory), the French Southern and Antarctic Lands (the Adélie Coast is the Antarctic portionof this French territory), Norway (Queen Maud Land and Peter I Island), the Ross Dependency (New Zealand), the Magallanes Region and the Chilean Antarctica Region (the Chilean Antarctic Territory) and the Argentinian province of Tierra del Fuego and the Antarctica and Southern Atlantic Islands (whose flag was created through a competition).

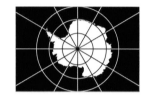

2002

is when the treaty organization created their flag. It represents the continent seen from the South Pole, the white standing out against a dark blue background scored with lines for parallels and meridians.

South of the 60th Parallel

Based on the seniority of their missions, the United Kingdom, Australia, New Zealand, France and Norway mutually acknowledge their defined areas from 1930 to 1950.

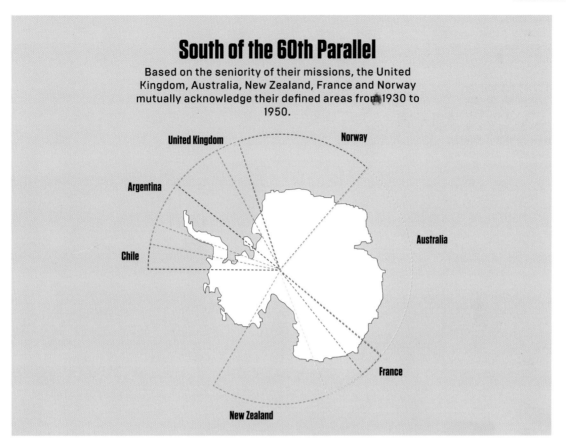

Allocated Territories

The Antarctic Treaty signed in 1961 does not force any state that controls an Antarctic territory to relinquish its sector, but it has frozen any new territorial claims. The flags below include territories located north and south of the 60th parallel.

British Antarctic Territory (United Kingdom)

Tierra del Fuego and Antarctica and Southern Atlantic Islands (Argentina)

Magallanes and Chilean Antarctica Region (Chilean Antarctic Territory, Chile)

Australian Antarctic Territory (Australia)

Ross Dependency (New Zealand)

French Southern and Antarctic Lands (France)

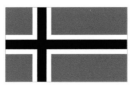

Queen Maud Land and Peter I Island (Norway)

The flags of the first 12 nations that signed the Antarctic Treaty are flown on the frozen continent: South Africa, Argentina, Australia, Belgium, Chile, United States, France, Japan, Norway, New Zealand, United Kingdom and Russia (USSR at that time).

INDIGENOUS PEOPLES

We are black on the red earth under the sun."
Motto of the Aboriginal Peoples of Australia

There are many flags used by cultural, historical and religious groups who want to affirm their identity and their heritage.

These flags are generally used to affirm a group's culture or shared language, rather than a claim to a specific territory (although some of these peoples do assert territorial claims). There are more than 80 Indigenous Peoples, i.e., the descendants of the first inhabitants of a region, who possess a flag. These groups have maintained a common language, and the majority continue to live within the same territory. Among them are the Berbers of North Africa, the Copts in Egypt and the Maasai of East Africa. The Ashanti of West Africa have kept the flag of their ancient kingdom. It features the Golden Stool, a symbol of unity, on a black background, with stripes of gold, associated with mineral wealth, and green, a symbol of tropical forests. There are also the flags of the Basques (Europe), the Maya (Central America), the Quechua (South America) and the many Indigenous Peoples of North America, including the Inuit (who inhabit northern Canada as well as Greenland). The flag of the Aboriginal Peoples in Australia, created in 1971, illustrates their motto: "We are black on the red earth under the sun." There are also many other flags associated with non-Indigenous ethnic groups who are united by their history or their religion, such as Afrikaners, Tartars, Romani, Druze, Sami and Acadians. African Americans and Arabs also identify themselves with a flag.

Aboriginal Peoples of Australia

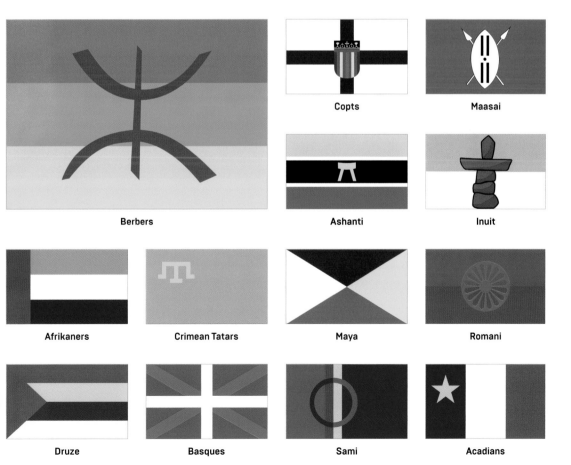

Berbers

Copts

Maasai

Ashanti

Inuit

Afrikaners

Crimean Tatars

Maya

Romani

Druze

Basques

Sami

Acadians

Indigenous Peoples of the Americas

Indigenous Peoples lived on the American continent before the arrival of European settlers. The colonization of the Americas led to massacres, numerous wars and the enslavement of a portion of the Indigenous population, leaving deep scars. In the 1960s, Indigenous Peoples began reclaiming their cultural, linguistic and political identity, and most created flags that recall strong symbols of their history and demonstrate their alliances. In the United States, the Pawnee, who originated in Nebraska and Kansas, today form the Pawnee Nation of Oklahoma. Their flag bears eight arrowheads that symbolize the battles lead by their people alongside settlers. In Canada, the flag of the Iroquois Confederacy was inspired by an ancient object, the Hiawatha Belt. Hiawatha is considered the founder of the Iroquois Confederacy, who united five tribes under the same banner, adding a sixth in 1722: the Seneca, Cayuga, Onondaga, Oneida, Tuscarora and Mohawk. The Iroquois used belts as adornment and currency, as well as to ratify treaties and validate alliances. Such is the case with the Hiawatha Belt, whose geometric motifs represent the five original tribes of the confederacy, bound together by a constitution. The Seneca are the keepers of the Western Door (at left), the Mohawk are the keepers of the Eastern Door (at right), and the Onondagas are the keepers of the Central Fire. Hiawatha's influence is widespread. In 1988, the United States Congress officially recognized the influence of the Six Nations on the country's political system and democratic principles.

22

Groups

A total of 22 groups (generally referred to as nations or tribes) of Indigenous Peoples are spread across the Americas.

Iroquois

The flag of the Iroquois Confederacy in Canada was inspired by the Hiawatha Belt, named after a hero who lived around 1400 and was both prophet and leader of the Onondaga and Mohawk Nations.

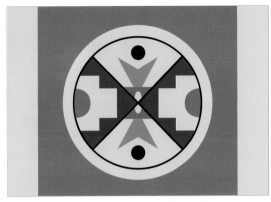

Eel Ground Natuaqanek (Canada)

Cheyenne (United States)

Innu (Canada)

Haida (Canada)

Sac and Fox (United States)

Arapaho (United States)

Mi'kmaq (Canada)

Oglala Sioux (United States)

Crow (United States)

Cherokee (United States)

Navajo (United States)

Pawnee (United States)

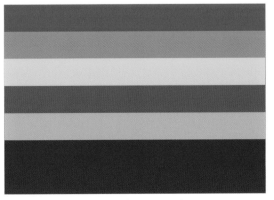

Quechua (Bolivia, Peru)

Indigenous Peoples of Colombia

Maya (Mexico, Guatemala)

Mapuche (Chile)

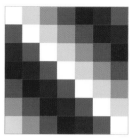

Qullasuyu Wiphala

Peoples of the Andes

In South America, the Andean Peoples have a checkered multicolor square flag called the Wiphala. Its name means "flag" in the language of the Aymara People. More than simply a flag, the Wiphala is the emblem of the unification of the Andean Peoples. It is flown during social and cultural celebrations in all Andean countries, particularly among the Aymara and Inca communities, who associate the flag with family celebrations. It also embodies their political claims. Its seven colors, arranged diagonally, recall the colors of the rainbow: red is for the earth, orange for community, yellow for strength and energy, white for wisdom, green for economic production, blue for the cosmos and infinity, and purple for politics. This flag did not exist at the time of the Incan Empire. It was created in 1944 to mark the unity of Andean Peoples, and its usage spread widely during the Indigenous movements of the 1970s in Bolivia, where it became the second official flag in 2009 and an emblem of the multinational country. There are now several regional variations of the flag, which alter the colors and their layout. The variations (at right) are named after the provinces of the ancient Inca Empire (for example, Bolivia is referred to as Qullasuyu).

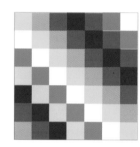

Kuntisuyu Wiphala

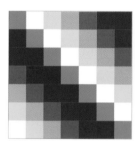

Antisuyu Wiphala

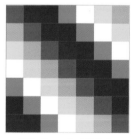

Chinchaysuhu Wiphala

La Paz, Bolivia (2016): Inauguration of a Wiphala housing complex project, decorated with a giant fresco by Bolivian artist Mamani Mamani.

CHAPTER 6

THE FLAG AS A UNIVERSAL MEDIUM

Flags are a powerful communication tool. Visible from far away, simple to use and easily changed around, they can be used to transmit information, dictate rules, warn against danger, protect humanitarian efforts and even threaten an adversary.

THE PRIDE FLAG

The rainbow flag, also called the pride flag, has become the symbol of the LGBTQ (lesbian, gay, bisexual, transgender and queer or questioning) community.

Created by American artist Gilbert Baker in 1978, the flag initially had eight colors, but a few were dropped when its mass production began in 1979: pink and turquoise disappeared, and indigo was replaced by royal blue.

This flag follows the order of the colors of the rainbow. According to Baker, red is for life, orange for healing, yellow for sunlight, green for nature, blue for harmony and purple for spirit. The pink symbolized sexuality, and turquoise symbolized art. Today, there are other flags associated with different sexual orientations and gender identities.

Life

Healing

Sunlight

Nature

Harmony

Spirit

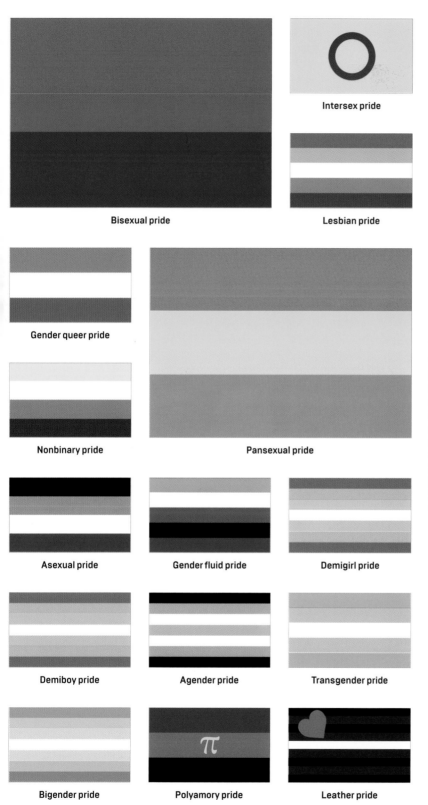

Intersex pride

Bisexual pride

Lesbian pride

Gender queer pride

Nonbinary pride

Pansexual pride

Asexual pride

Gender fluid pride

Demigirl pride

Demiboy pride

Agender pride

Transgender pride

Bigender pride

Polyamory pride

Leather pride

Pride

Several pride flags exist. These standards are displayed to recognize a particular sexual orientation, gender identity, romantic attachment, relationship or sexual practice. Some of these flags also have several variations.

THE COMMON GOOD: NGOS

A non-governmental organization is a public-interest non-profit association. It is defined by its political independence.

An NGO can operate at the local, national or international. One of the most well-known NGOs is the International Committee of the Red Cross (ICRC), which was established by Henri Dunant following the Battle of Solferino (1859). It is often considered the forebearer of modern NGOs. However, instances of international mutual assistance certainly existed before that time. For example, at the request of the United States, emergency humanitarian response efforts were undertaken in Venezuela following an earthquake and during the Irish Famine. Moreover, wealthy nurse Florence Nightingale organized medical teams that were active during the Crimean War (1853–1855), the American Civil War (1861–1865) and the Franco-Prussian War of 1870. During the Second World War, charitable organizations spread worldwide. However, it was the United Nations that defined the concept of an NGO, in order to include civilians in its projects. Throughout the following decades, NGOs progressively evolved and specialized. While many remain completely neutral and apolitical, others are founded on spiritual values, such as Catholic Relief and Islamic Relief.

The ship Aquarius was chartered by SOS Méditerranée, in partnership with Doctors of the World and Doctors Without Borders, to rescue migrants.

4

4 Main Categories

There are four main categories of NGOs, based on their purpose and their work: humanitarian relief, environmental protection, human rights protection and development.

Doctors Without Borders (MSF)

Greenpeace

Amnesty International

Action Against Hunger

Doctors of the World

ONE

World Wildlife Fund (WWF)

Handicap International (Humanity and Inclusion)

Friends of the Earth International

CARE

Human Rights Watch

Oxfam

Sea Shepherd

Save the Children

The Red Cross

Number 1 in the World

The International Red Cross and Red Crescent Movement is the largest group of humanitarian organizations in the world.

The flag with a red cross on a white background was created in 1863 to protect volunteer nurses who went onto battlefields to help the wounded. In 1864, following the First Geneva Convention and in the interest of better helping wounded soldiers, the red cross symbol became the single distinctive sign of all military medical personnel as well as military hospitals and ambulances. Today, it is combined with the red crescent as well as the lion and red sun on a white background — all three are signs of protection given to people and goods in the framework of the Geneva Convention. According to Article 38, Section 1538 of the convention, the red cross and related symbols allow their beneficiaries to go onto battlefields to carry out their humanitarian mission: "It bears witness to the totally inoffensive character of the persons and objects that it designates, as well as to the impartial, useful and orderly nature of their humanitarian task, and in return, it grants them immunity. Thus it should be displayed in good faith and in accordance with the prescribed conditions, deployed widely wherever possible and permanently under a strict control of the conditions of its use."

These symbols can also be used in times of peace to indicate that a person or good is connected to the Red Cross and Red Crescent Movement. Thus, their use is strictly limited and codified so that these symbols of protection remain a guarantee of safety for those who venture unarmed into a conflict with the sole purpose of helping the wounded, sick, and threatened or abandoned civilians.

The Red Cross flag flies
beside the UN flag in a
Rwandan refugee camp
in Zaire, in 1994.

THE MARITIME ALPHABET

Since 1969, all navies around the world communicate with each other using an international code, composed of an alphabet and several combinations.

This international code is transmitted by "flag-hoist communication" using ensign and pennants. Each flag corresponds to a number (pennants) or a letter (ensigns) to form phrases that everyone can understand or coded messages that can only be deciphered by the intended party. There is also a simplified code in which each flag is assigned a specific meaning related to ship maneuvers. When combined in pairs, these flags take on different meanings.

The NATO phonetic alphabet, created in 1959 and recognized by the International Telecommunication Union (ITU) and the International Civil Aviation Organization (ICAO), is used for maritime signaling. In this alphabet, each letter is represented by the initial letter of a word, for example Bravo for the letter B. This prevents confusion between letters that sound the same. NATO also has a code that is classified as "confidential defense," which is used by military ships to exchange top-secret messages.

A–Z

The Phonetic Alphabet

Signals use the NATO phonetic alphabet to spell out the letter of each word. However, simplified messages can be sent via ensigns.

A (Alfa)

I have a diver down. Keep well clear at slow speed.

B (Bravo)

I am loading, unloading or carrying dangerous goods.

C (Charlie)

Yes (*affirmative response or the significance of the previous group should be read in the affirmative*).

D (Delta)

Keep clear of me; I am maneuvering with difficulty.

E (Echo)

I am altering my course to starboard.

F (Foxtrot)

I am disabled; communicate with me.

G (Golf)

1. I require a pilot;
2. (*By a fishing vessel*) I am hauling nets.

H (Hotel)

I have a pilot on board.

I (India)

I am altering my course to port.

J (Juliett)

Keep well clear of me;I am on fire and have dangerous cargo on board, or I am leaking dangerous cargo.

K (Kilo)

I wish to communicate with you.

L (Lima)

You should stop your vessel immediately.

M (Mike)

My vessel is stopped and making no way.

N (November)

No (*negative response or the significance of the previous group should be read in the negative*).

O (Oscar)

Man overboard.

P (Papa)

(In harbor) All persons should report on board as the vessel is about to set sail.

Q (Quebec)

My vessel is "healthy" and I request free practice.

R (Romeo)

Procedure signal

S (Sierra)

I am operating astern propulsion.

T (Tango)

(For a fishing vessel) Keep clear of me; I am engaged in pair trawling.

U (Uniform)

You are running into danger.

V (Victor)

I require assistance.

W (Whiskey)

I require medical assistance.

X (X-ray)

Stop your maneuvers and watch for my signals.

Y (Yankee)

I am dragging my anchor.

Z (Zulu)

1. I require a tug;

2: *(By a fishing vessel)* I am shooting nets.

Two-Letter Combinations

Two-letter signals are used to deliver additional messages. There is a plethora of combinations. The most important combination is November + Charlie: "I am in distress and require immediate assistance."

NC
I am in distress.

ED
Your distress signal has been understood.

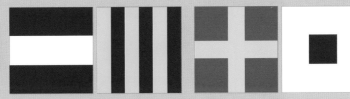

JG
I have run aground.

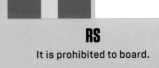

RS
It is prohibited to board.

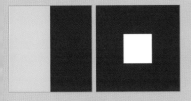

KP
Tow me to port.

NA
Navigation is prohibited.

QL
Go back.

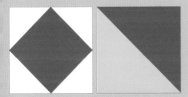

FO
I will remain close to you.

KN
I cannot tow you.

PM
Follow my wake.

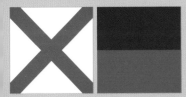

VE
I am disinfecting my ship.

JB
There is risk of explosion.

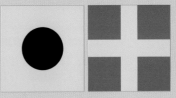

IR
Stay away.

Maritime Ensigns

An ensign is a flag hoisted aloft or at the back of a ship. It is flown on the flagpole located at the back of the ship when in port or anchored and on the mizzenmast when at sea. It signals the ship's nationality and acts as a kind of license plate. Merchant navies use civil ensigns, public services (such as customs, coast guards and postal services) use state ensigns and navies use naval ensigns. A jack flag is added to the stem of docked or anchored war ships. A flag of authority is also added to the flagship's stem to communicate the rank of the fleet's commanding officer. Many countries use a single ensign, which duplicates the national flag, for all of their ships.

By contrast, the United Kingdom has three different ensigns: the Red Ensign, which has a red background and Union Jack in the upper-left canton, is reserved for their

Red Ensign

Civil ensign of the Isle of Man

The United Kingdom has three maritime ensigns. The Red Ensign is the foundation of the civil ensigns of the Isle of Man and Guernsey as well as the Bermuda flag.

Blue Ensign

Civil ensign of Guernsey

White Ensign

Flag of Bermuda

merchant navy; the Blue Ensign, which has a blue background, is used by public service ships and certain yacht members who belong to long-established yacht clubs; and the White Ensign, which has a white background and is also called the Saint George's Ensign because of its red cross, is used by the British Royal Navy. The Guernsey, the Isle of Man and Bermuda added their blazon to the Red Ensign to create their flags.

On merchant ships, the ensign is the national flag of the country in which the boat is registered. In 2017, approximately 70% of commercial fleets flew an ensign different from the ship's country of ownership. In addition to the national ensign, it is customary for each ship to display a courtesy flag displaying the country where it is located; ships that do not fly such flags may be refused entry at ports.

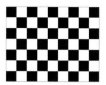

Finish line

Hazard

Hazard has been cleared

Warning (unsportsmanlike behavior)

Disqualification

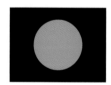

Dangerous mechanical issue for the car indicated

Track is slippery

SPORTS FLAGS

Motor racing features some of the most recognized sports-related flags. What could be simpler than colored flags to communicate information to race car drivers who are blinded by a dusty track?

Racing flags were thus born. Yellow, red or blue flags are waved from the side of the track to warn competitors of danger, stop the race or tell a driver to give way to an approaching car. However, the most iconic flag, the one that every driver dreams of seeing lowered in front of them, is the black and white checkered flag that announces the arrival of the winner and the end of a race. A legend traces its design to the first 24 Hours of Le Mans race, in 1923, when the track marshal allegedly picked up the chess board on which he'd been playing and waved it to mark the winner's arrival. However, the flag existed long before then and can be seen in photos dating from the 1900s. While its origins remain uncertain, it seems to have been borrowed from other sports. For example, the organizers of a cycling race in France in 1860 wore checkered uniforms so they could be easily visible from a distance. Further, during horseracing events in the American Midwest, there was a tradition of checkered tablecloths being waved to indicate to the public that the race was over and the picnic was being served — on those checkered tablecloths, of course!

Beach Flags

"Swim Here"

In Australia, a paradise for surfers and swimmers, safety is taken very seriously. Zones supervised by lifeguards are always marked with two red and yellow flags, indicating the start and end of the swimming zone.

Flags play an important role in all kinds of sports. Flags with a team's colors or logo are brandished by crowds to show their support. Different sports also often use relatively similar flags. For example, the most common colors for racing flags — green, yellow and red — are also used for beach flags. These triangular flags attached to poles on beaches provide important safety information to swimmers and surfers: green indicates it is safe to swim; orange or yellow signal that there are hazards but supervised swimming is permitted; red indicates swimming and other water activities are prohibited; and purple signals danger from pollution or marine creatures, such as jellyfish. Blue pennants outline the supervised swimming area and green flags with a red circle mark the zone set aside for surfing and other water activities. The black and yellow striped flags indicate the entire supervised zone. Finally, altough the black and white checkered flag is known to mark the end of a motor race, it is also used on mountains to warn skiers and snowboarders of the risk of avalanches.

Motorcycle Sports

The flags used in motorcycle sports all bear a cross:: a red cross on a white background indicates rain, a white cross on a red background signals that a safety vehicle is on the track, and a black cross on a yellow background indicates the final lap of the race.

Flags and the Olympic Games

Even though the Olympics are a major international sporting event, certain countries are not represented at them. For example, Vatican City has never participated, and Russia was banned in 2018 after a sanction from the International Olympics Committee, following a doping scandal. However, Russian athletes were able to compete under the Olympic flag. Conversely, participating nations are not always members of the UN or recognized as sovereign states by the entire United Nations. Here are the flags of some nations that may not be recognized as such but have participated in Olympic Games nonetheless.

Olympic flag

Unified Korea

Cook Islands

Cayman Islands

British Virgin Islands

Chinese Taipei (the name and flag under which Taiwan competes at the Olympics)

Bermuda

Puerto Rico

Kosovo

United States Virgin Islands

Guam

Aruba

American Samoa

Hong Kong (China)

Palestine

PIRATES

Pirates would fly ensigns to terrorize the crews of merchant ships, whose cargo they coveted. That's why they often feature symbols and images associated with death.

Skeletons, bones, skulls and bloody hearts combined with swords and lit cannonballs are the most common motifs on pirate flags. Another popular motif is the hourglass, which symbolizes that time is running out and death is near. Englishman Edward Teach (1680—1718), better known as known as Blackbeard, was one of North America's most notorious pirates. Despite his reputation, he actually preferred cunning over force. Feared for his acts of looting at sea, he took great care to maintain a terrifying image by stroking his long black beard and lighting cannon fuses under his hat during his assaults. He died in combat. His ensign, which largely contributed to his reputation, displayed the devil's skeleton on a black background. The devil held a spear ready to pierce a red heart in his left hand and either a glass for toasting or an hourglass in his right hand.

In the 18th century, the so-called filibusters who operated in the Antilles adopted a unique ensign with a skull overlying two crossbones. At the time of an attack, the pirates would fly either the black ensign to encourage their adversaries to surrender without fighting or a red ensign to announce that they were about to board and no mercy would be shown. Some pirates preferred to hide behind flags of convenience taken from defeated ships. Unsuspecting merchant ships would thereby let them approach more easily. In 1720, English pirate Bartholomew Roberts sunk a slave ship and then flew that ship's Dutch ensign. He was subsequently able to capture 14 French ships who wanted to buy slaves from him! To blend in, some merchant ships did not hesitate to fly a flag of convenience in the hopes of avoiding privateers who would attack the fleets of countries who were at war with their homeland.

Flying a false flag

was a very effective way to avoid adversaries or board a ship by surprise.

Pavillon de R:as de S.ᵗ Maur, long de 22 pieds 9 pouces & large de 14 pieds 9 pouces.

Ensign of Captain Jean Thomas Dulaien, who sailed the pirate ship *Merciless*.

Ensign of Jacquotte
Delahaye

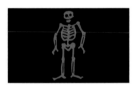

Ensign of Edward Low

Ensign of Henry Every

Ensign of Emmanuel Wynne

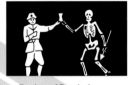

Ensign of Bartholomew
Roberts

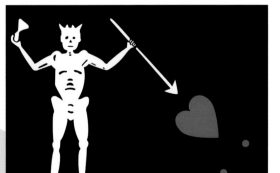

Ensign of Edward "Blackbeard" Teach

Ensign of Jack Rackham

Ensign of Stede Bonnet

Ensign of Thomas Tew

OPINIONS AND ACTIVISM

In politics, colors are a very visual way to affirm an idea or defend a cause because they can deliver a message at a single glance.

Since the 19th century, red has been associated with socialism and communism: It is the color of the blood of the workers who fought for their freedom. Unions have often preserved this notion of class struggle by using flags with a red background. Black, meanwhile, illustrates anarchism; various flags associated with anarchistic movements are divided in two by a diagonal line with the lower section in black. Black can also refer to mourning. One such example is the logo and

flag of Extinction Rebellion. Green, the color of nature in full bloom, is often used to symbolize the fight for the environment and can be associated with the Green Party. Purple denotes feminism, since it is a mix of pink, associated with females, and blue, associated with males. It was the color worn by the suffragettes at the end of the 19th century and returned to the forefront with the feminist movements of the 1970s. Political flags also use striking symbols to communicate their message. Thus, the five-point star continues to be featured on the flags of communist and socialist countries. It refers to the five continents, whose workers unite in the fight for freedom. In Vietnam, it also symbolizes the union of laborers, soldiers, peasants, youth and intellectuals in that fight.

Extinction Rebellion

The flag and logo of the Extinction Rebellion environmental movement is black to symbolize endangered species. Its symbol, the hourglass at the center of a circle representing Earth, refers to the time running out for species on the verge of extinction. According to the UN, a species becomes extinct every 8 minutes.

Feminism (variations exist)

Anarchism (after 1968)

Veganism

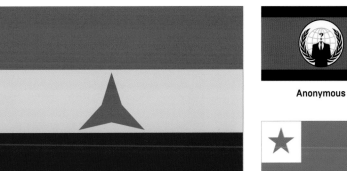

International Brigades (1936–1938)

Anonymous

Esperanto movement

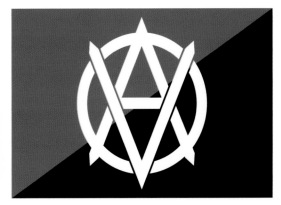

Vegananarchism

Suffragettes (variations exist)

CHAPTER 7

AN OVERVIEW OF FLAGS

An inventory of all the flags that have existed and currently exist would be endless. However, this selection of a few hundred flags does provide a substantive overview of world history in the 20th and 21st centuries — a brief glimpse into how flags and the countries they represent can be compared and contrasted.

A Family Resemblance

When side by side, certain flags look very similar!

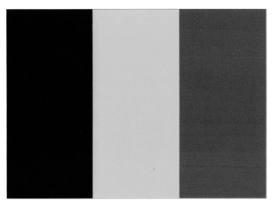

Chad

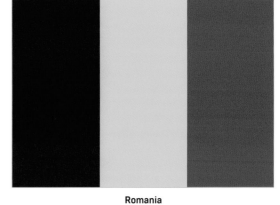

Romania

Australia

New Zealand

Cook Islands

Tuvalu

Senegal

Cameroon

Turkey

Tunisia

Bangladesh

Japan

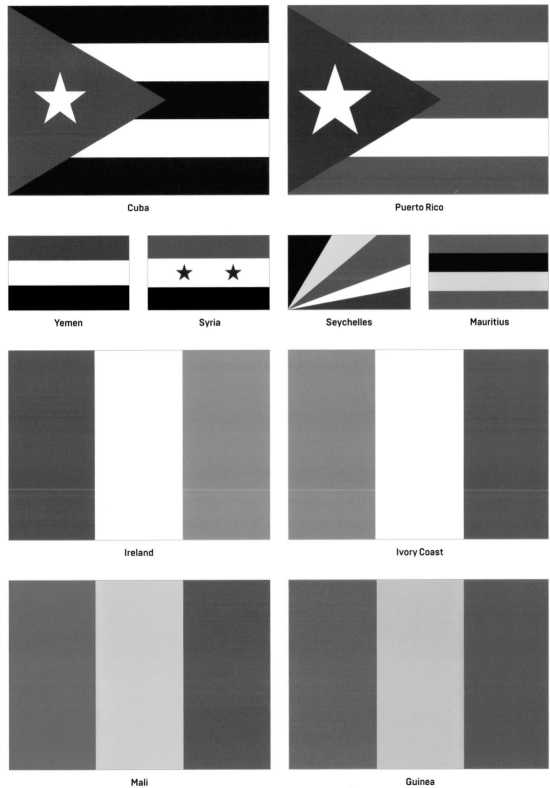

Cuba

Puerto Rico

Yemen

Syria

Seychelles

Mauritius

Ireland

Ivory Coast

Mali

Guinea

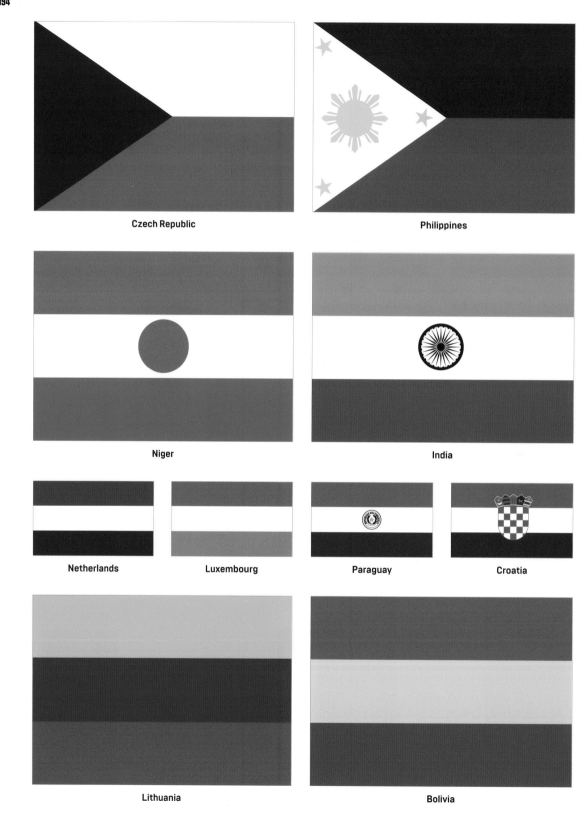

Czech Republic

Philippines

Niger

India

Netherlands

Luxembourg

Paraguay

Croatia

Lithuania

Bolivia

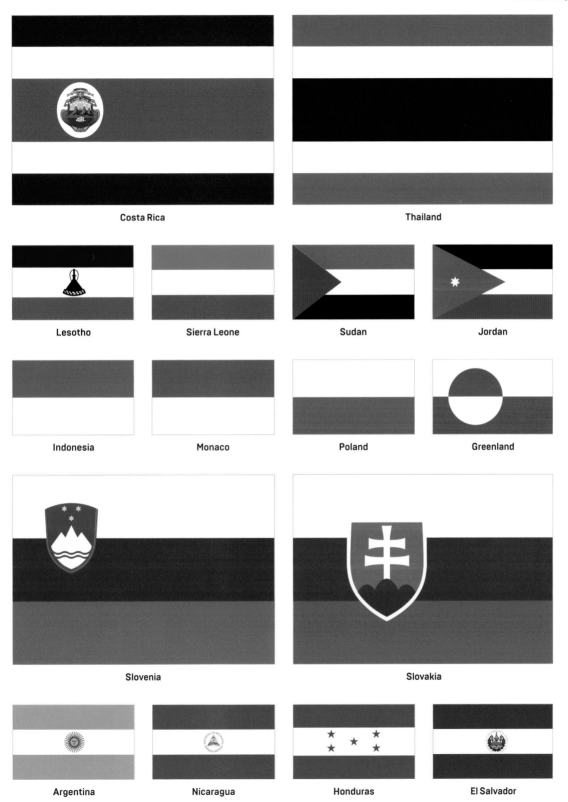

Costa Rica

Thailand

Lesotho

Sierra Leone

Sudan

Jordan

Indonesia

Monaco

Poland

Greenland

Slovenia

Slovakia

Argentina

Nicaragua

Honduras

El Salvador

Elaborate Flags

Some flags have details so small that they are hard to detect and require a closer look.

Ecuador

Haiti

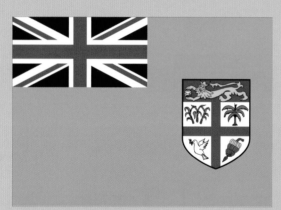

Fiji

San Marino

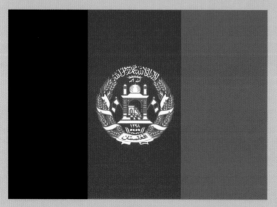

Afghanistan

Dominican Republic

Turkmenistan

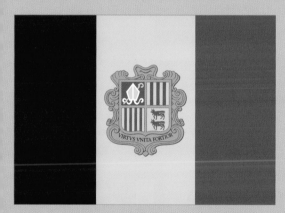

Andorra

Brunei

Moldova

Egypt

Winning Combinations

Particular arrangements, designs and forms are common among several national flags. Here are the three most popular compositions.

NUMBER 1: THREE HORIZONTAL STRIPES

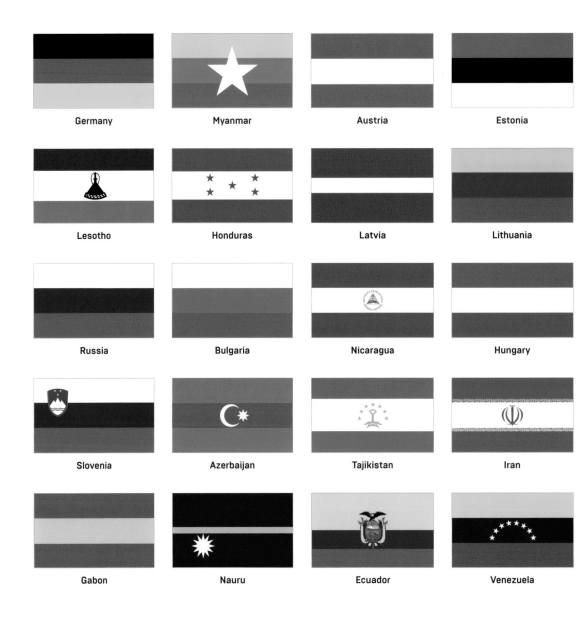

Germany

Myanmar

Austria

Estonia

Lesotho

Honduras

Latvia

Lithuania

Russia

Bulgaria

Nicaragua

Hungary

Slovenia

Azerbaijan

Tajikistan

Iran

Gabon

Nauru

Ecuador

Venezuela

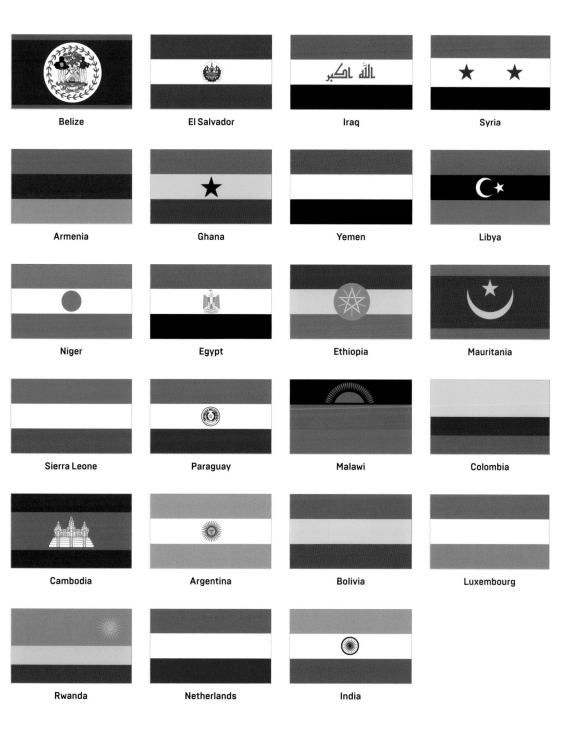

Belize	El Salvador	Iraq	Syria
Armenia	Ghana	Yemen	Libya
Niger	Egypt	Ethiopia	Mauritania
Sierra Leone	Paraguay	Malawi	Colombia
Cambodia	Argentina	Bolivia	Luxembourg
Rwanda	Netherlands	India	

200

NUMBER 2:
Vertical Stripes

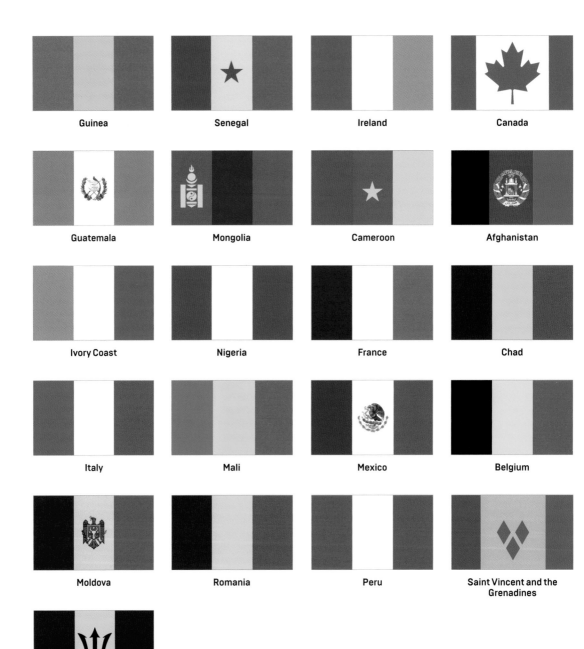

Guinea

Senegal

Ireland

Canada

Guatemala

Mongolia

Cameroon

Afghanistan

Ivory Coast

Nigeria

France

Chad

Italy

Mali

Mexico

Belgium

Moldova

Romania

Peru

Saint Vincent and the Grenadines

Barbados

NUMBER 3:
A Triangle on the Hoist

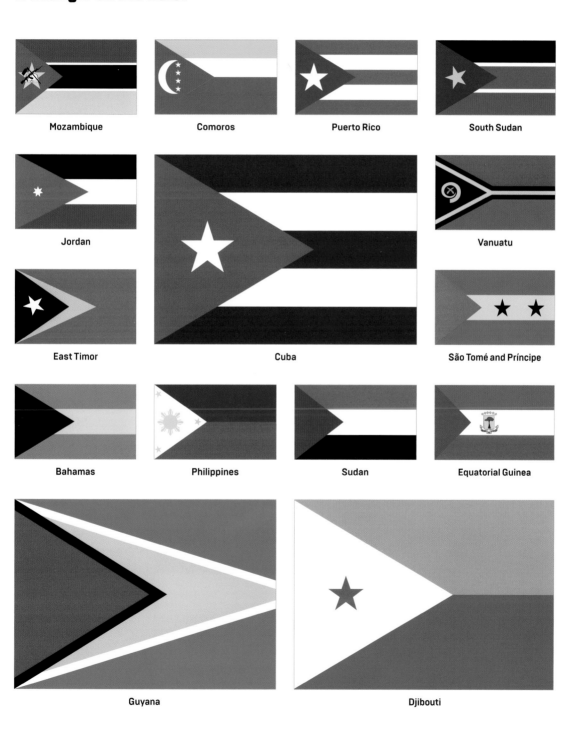

Mozambique

Comoros

Puerto Rico

South Sudan

Jordan

Vanuatu

East Timor

Cuba

São Tomé and Príncipe

Bahamas

Philippines

Sudan

Equatorial Guinea

Guyana

Djibouti

Winning Motifs

Among the various motifs that appear on national and regional flags, one type has really taken off: the symbols linked to celestial bodies (stars, crescent moons, suns and constellations).

STAR AND CRESCENT MOON

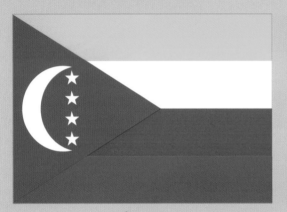

Comoros

Uzbekistan

Aruba (Netherlands)

Angola

Morocco

Ethiopia

Ghana

Guinea-Bissau

São Tomé and Príncipe

Honduras

Jordan

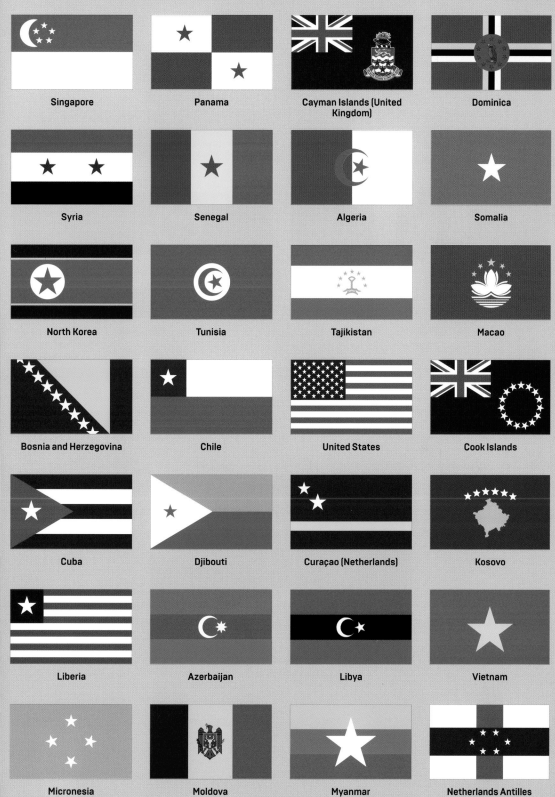

Singapore

Panama

Cayman Islands (United Kingdom)

Dominica

Syria

Senegal

Algeria

Somalia

North Korea

Tunisia

Tajikistan

Macao

Bosnia and Herzegovina

Chile

United States

Cook Islands

Cuba

Djibouti

Curaçao (Netherlands)

Kosovo

Liberia

Azerbaijan

Libya

Vietnam

Micronesia

Moldova

Myanmar

Netherlands Antilles (Netherlands)

SUN

Moldova

Costa Rica

Kiribati

North Macedonia

Kazakhstan

Kurdistan

Uruguay

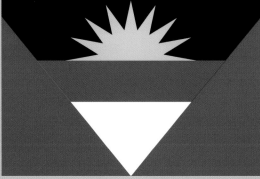

Antigua and Barbuda

Nepal

Rwanda

Republic of China (Taiwan)

Namibia

Argentina

Kyrgyzstan

Malawi

CONSTELLATIONS

Papua New Guinea

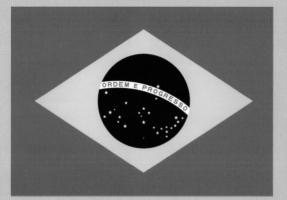

Brazil

Magallanes and Chilean Antarctica Region (Chile)

Solomon Islands

Tokelau (New Zealand)

Tierra del Fuego (Argentina)

Christmas Island (Australia)

New Zealand

Australia

Alaska (United States)

New South Wales (Australia)

Samoa

Niue

Australian Capital Territory (Australia)

Northern Territory (Australia))

Unique Flags

All national flags are unique, but some add a special detail that help make them really stand out.

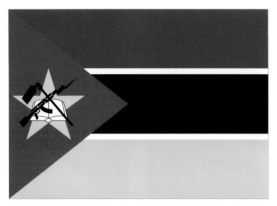

Mozambique (only flag that features a contemporary weapon)

Nepal (unique shape and proportions)

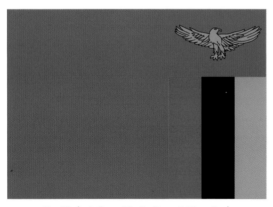

Zambia (only flag with a bottom-right canton)

Paraguay (only current flag that is double sided)

Denmark (oldest flag to remain unchanged)

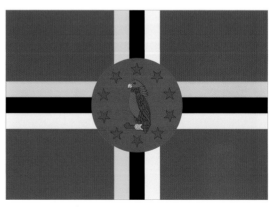

Dominica (only flag that features the color purple)

Cambodia (only current flag that features a building outside of a blazon or coat of arms)

Cyprus and Kosovo (only two flags to display the shape of their country)

Former Flags

Countries have disappeared on every continent. Some were absorbed by other countries and others were grouped together to form new countries.*

Katanga (Democratic Republic of the Congo)

State of Rhodesia (Zimbabwe)

People's Republic of Zanzibar (Tanzania)

Orange Free State (South Africa)

Republic of Formosa (Republic of China / Taiwan)

Mughal Empire (India)

South African Republic of Transvaal (South Africa)

Kingdom of Tanganyika (Tanzania)

Hyderabad (India)

Los Altos (Guatemala and Mexico)

Kingdom of Bora Bora (French Polynesia, France)

Kingdom of Scotland (United Kingdom)

West Indies Federation (Antilles)

People's Democratic Republic of Yemen (Yemen)

*The country in which the territory is now located is indicated in parentheses.

Meanwhile, other countries have been divided to form several different countries.

Czechoslovakia

Ottoman Empire

Great Korean Empire

USSR

Austria-Hungary

Federal Republic of Central America

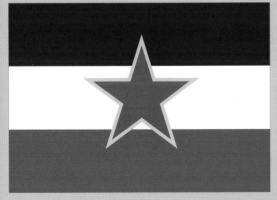

Socialist Federal Republic of Yugoslavia

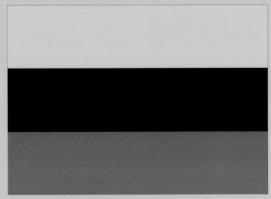

Transcaucasian Democratic Federative Republic

Indigenous Peoples

Indigenous Peoples celebrate their origins and culture through their flags.

AFRICA

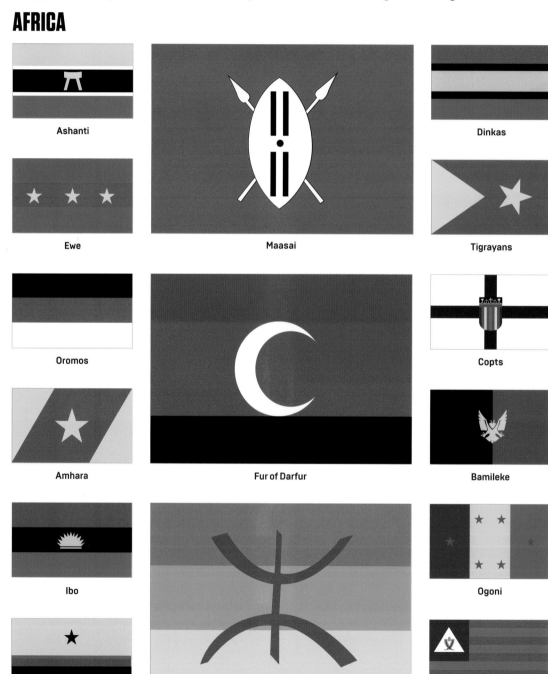

Ashanti

Dinkas

Ewe

Maasai

Tigrayans

Oromos

Copts

Amhara

Fur of Darfur

Bamileke

Ibo

Ogoni

Toubou-Gorane

Berbers

Bubi

AMERICA

Indigenous Peoples of
Colombia

Mapuche-Tehuelche

Innu

Inuit

Iroquois

Mi'kmaq

Eel Ground Natuaqanek

Anishinabe

Haida

Navajo

Taino

Garifuna

Cherokee

Maya

Sac and Fox

Arapaho

Cheyenne

Oglala Sioux

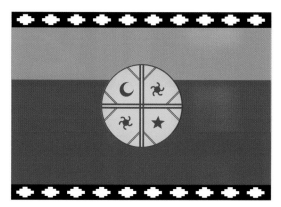

Mapuche

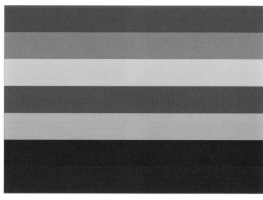

Quechua

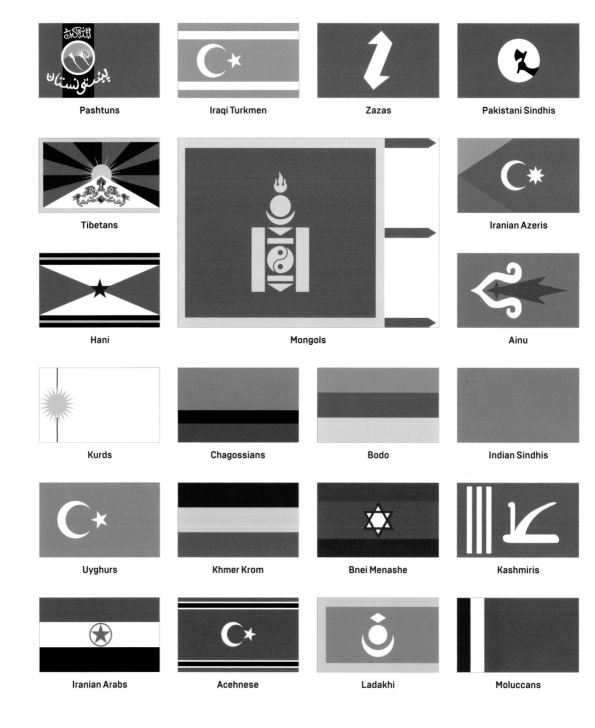

ASIA

Pashtuns

Iraqi Turkmen

Zazas

Pakistani Sindhis

Tibetans

Iranian Azeris

Hani

Mongols

Ainu

Kurds

Chagossians

Bodo

Indian Sindhis

Uyghurs

Khmer Krom

Bnei Menashe

Kashmiris

Iranian Arabs

Acehnese

Ladakhi

Moluccans

OCEANIA

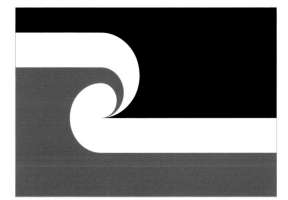

Maori

Indigenous French Polynesians

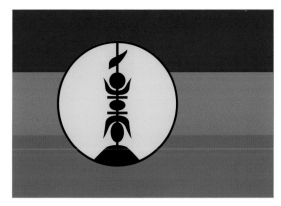

Kanaks

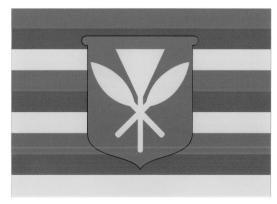

Hawaiian Polynesians

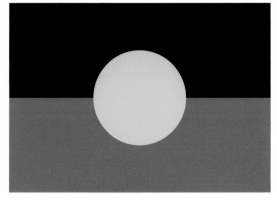

Australian Aboriginals

Indigenous Papua New Guineans

Ethnic Populations

These populations share a common ancestry, culture or way of life.

AMERICAS

Pan-African flag (1920)

Acadians

Franco-Ténois

Franco-Albertans

Franco-Americans

Franco-Ontarians

Métis (variant)

Métis (variant)

Francophones of
Newfoundland and Labrador

Cajuns

MIDDLE EAST

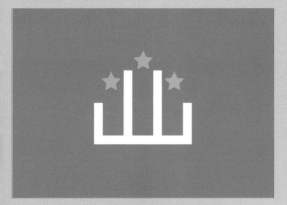

Kumyks

Druze

Meskhetians

Adjarians

Syriac Arameans

Assyrians (Assyro-Chaldeans)

EUROPE

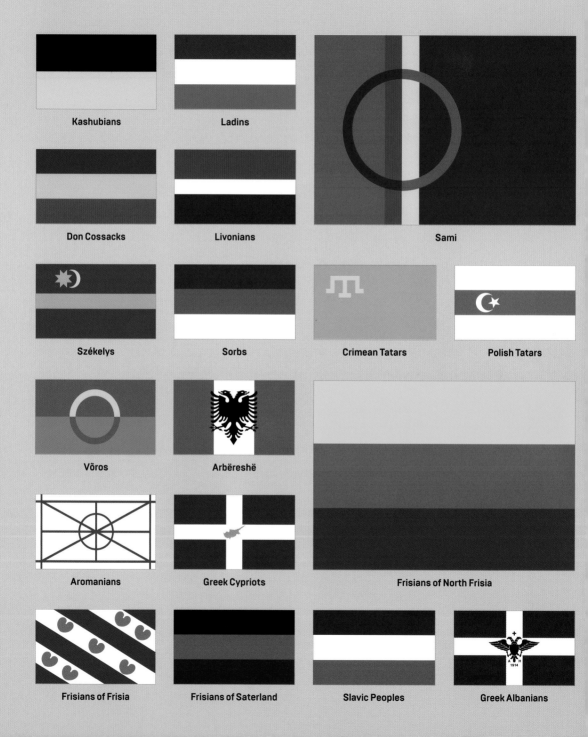

Kashubians

Ladins

Don Cossacks

Livonians

Sami

Székelys

Sorbs

Crimean Tatars

Polish Tatars

Võros

Arbëreshë

Aromanians

Greek Cypriots

Frisians of North Frisia

Frisians of Frisia

Frisians of Saterland

Slavic Peoples

Greek Albanians

OTHERS

Afrikaners

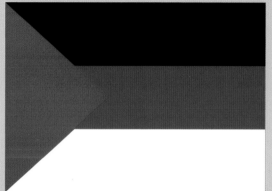

Pan-Arabs

Romani

Intergovernmental Organizations

Alliances among nations add another layer to global geopolitics.

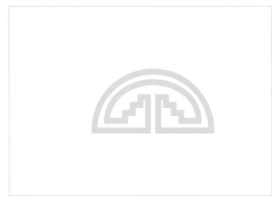

United Nations

Andean Community of Nations

Caribbean Community

Central American Integration System

Southern Common Market

Union of South American Nations

Eastern Caribbean States

North Atlantic Treaty Organization

Organization of American States

Organization of the Petroleum Exporting Countries

African Union

East African Community

Southern African Development Community

Arab League

Gulf Cooperation Council

Association of Southeast
Asian Nations

Pacific Community

Confederation of United Tribes of New Zealand

Community of Portuguese-Speaking Countries

Nordic Council

International Organisation of
La Francophonie

European Free Trade
Association

Central Commission for
Navigation of the Rhine

Countries in 1900

This list of the world's major countries in 1900 shows that over a century ago, there were barely more than 50.

Paraguay

Argentina

Australia

Belgium

Bolivia

Brazil

Bulgaria

Chile

China

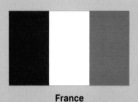

Costa Rica

Denmark

Germany

Ecuador

France

Greece

Great Britain

Guatemala

Haiti

Italy

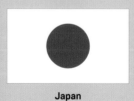

Japan

Canada

Colombia

Congo

Korea

Crete

Cuba	Liberia	Morocco	Mexico
Monaco	Montenegro	Netherlands	Norway
Ottoman Empire	Austria-Hungary	Peru	Portugal
Persia (Iran)	Romania	Russia	El Salvador
Dominican Republic	Sweden	Switzerland	Serbia
Siam	Spain	Tunisia	Uruguay
Venezuela	United States of America	Panama	Nicaragua

The History of a Flag

Following political changes, the flags of certain countries have evolved many, many times! Here are the "winners" of each continent. The prize, however, goes to the United States, which has introduced 27 versions of the Stars and Stripes!

VENEZUELA

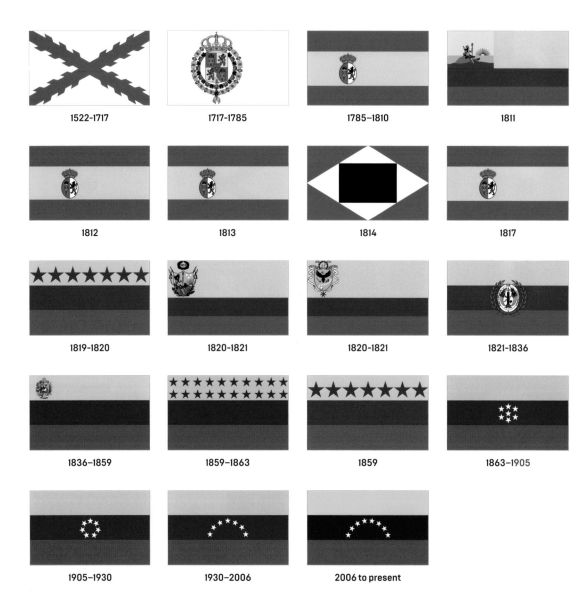

1522-1717

1717-1785

1785–1810

1811

1812

1813

1814

1817

1819-1820

1820-1821

1820-1821

1821-1836

1836–1859

1859–1863

1859

1863–1905

1905–1930

1930–2006

2006 to present

THE UNITED STATES

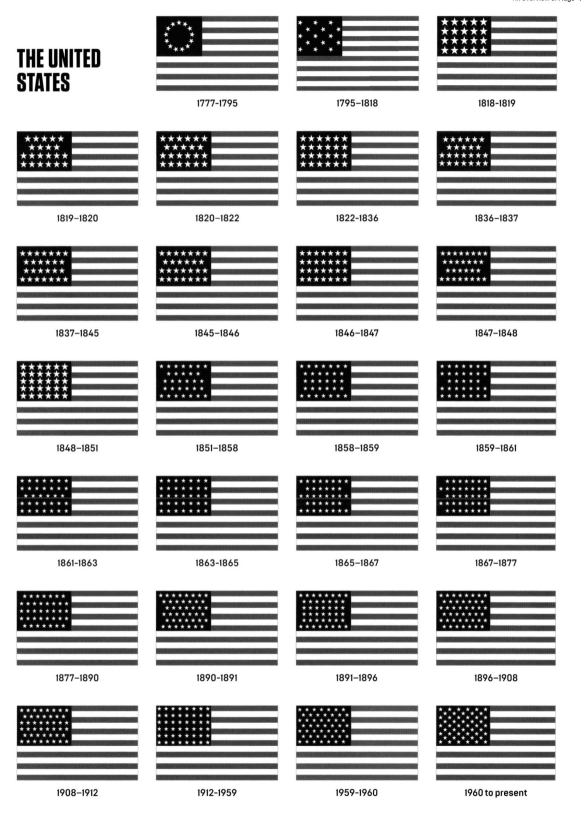

1777–1795

1795–1818

1818–1819

1819–1820

1820–1822

1822–1836

1836–1837

1837–1845

1845–1846

1846–1847

1847–1848

1848–1851

1851–1858

1858–1859

1859–1861

1861–1863

1863–1865

1865–1867

1867–1877

1877–1890

1890–1891

1891–1896

1896–1908

1908–1912

1912–1959

1959–1960

1960 to present

AFGHANISTAN

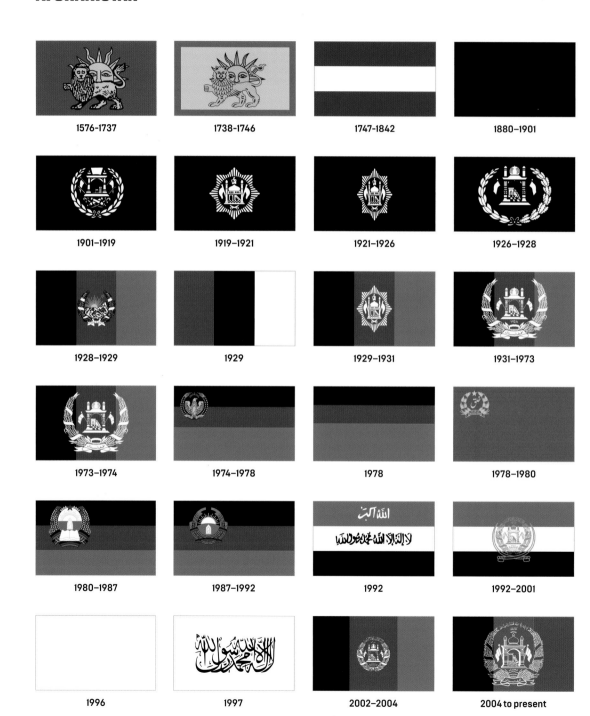

1576-1737	1738-1746	1747-1842	1880–1901
1901–1919	1919–1921	1921–1926	1926–1928
1928–1929	1929	1929–1931	1931–1973
1973–1974	1974–1978	1978	1978–1980
1980–1987	1987–1992	1992	1992–2001
1996	1997	2002–2004	2004 to present

EQUATORIAL GUINEA

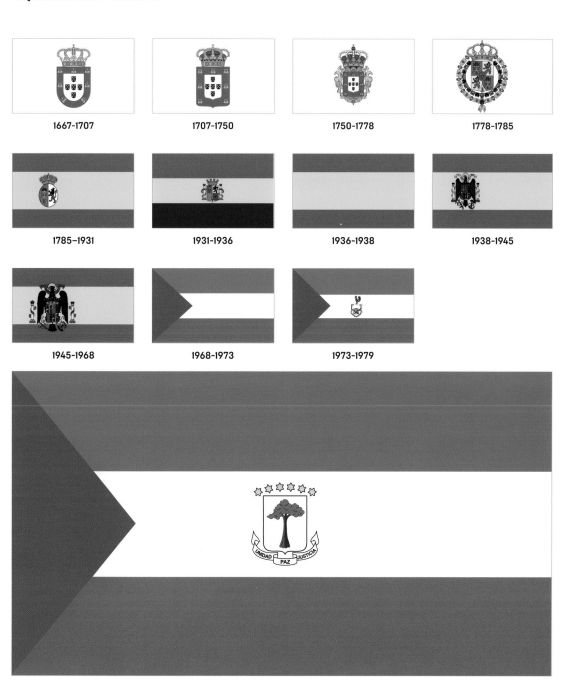

1667-1707

1707-1750

1750-1778

1778-1785

1785–1931

1931-1936

1936-1938

1938-1945

1945-1968

1968-1973

1973-1979

1979 to present

BOSNIA AND HERZEGOVINA

1453-1844

1844-1878

1878

1878–1908

1908–1918

1918–1941

1941–1945

1946-1992

1946–1992

1992–1998

1998 to present

Countries of the World Today

In 2020, more than 200 countries are recognized as independent states.

ASIA

North Korea

South Korea

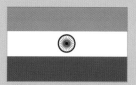
India

Nepal

Mongolia

China

Bangladesh

Myanmar

Japan

Singapore

Indonesia

East Timor

Philippines

Malaysia

Maldives

Cambodia

Vietnam

Thailand

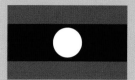
Laos

Brunei

Republic of China (Taiwan)

Bhutan

Sri Lanka

OCEANIA

Australia

New Zealand

Marshall Islands

Papua New Guinea

Nauru

Tuvalu

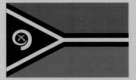

Vanuatu

Samoa

Kiribati

Solomon Islands

Fiji

Tonga

Niue

Cook Islands

Palau

Micronesia

Oman

MIDDLE EAST AND CENTRAL ASIA

Uzbekistan

Turkmenistan

Afghanistan

Georgia

Azerbaijan

Tajikistan

Pakistan

Turkey

Iraq

Iran

Saudi Arabia

Syria

Armenia

Yemen

Israel

Lebanon

United Arab Emirates

Jordan

Palestine

Qatar

Bahrain

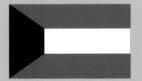

Kuwait

Kazakhstan

Kyrgyzstan

EUROPE

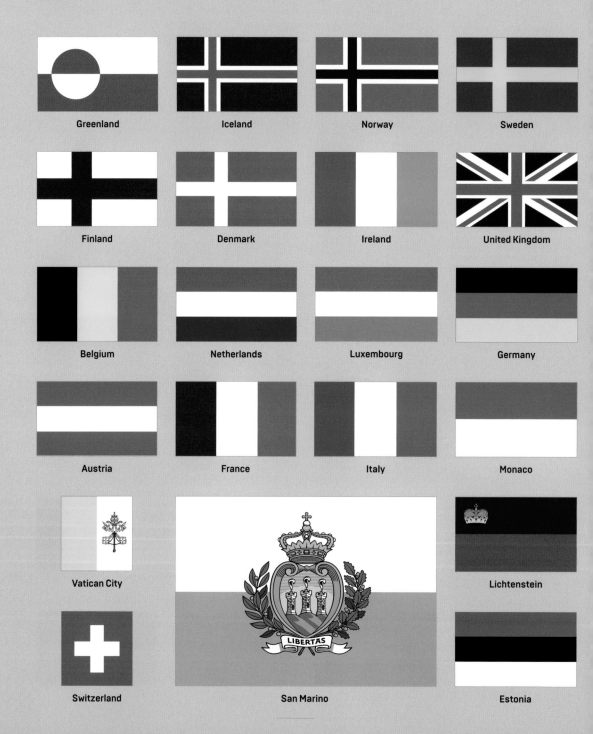

Greenland

Iceland

Norway

Sweden

Finland

Denmark

Ireland

United Kingdom

Belgium

Netherlands

Luxembourg

Germany

Austria

France

Italy

Monaco

Vatican City

San Marino

Lichtenstein

Switzerland

Estonia

Spain	Andorra	Portugal	Greece
Cyprus	Malta	Lithuania	Czech Republic
Slovakia	Poland	Russia	Bulgaria
Moldova	Belarus	Hungary	Romania
Ukraine	Montenegro	Kosovo	Albania
Croatia	Bosnia and Herzegovina	Serbia	Slovenia
North Macedonia	Latvia		

AFRICA

Morocco

Algeria

Tunisia

Libya

Niger

Chad

Eritrea

Ethiopia

Somalia

Mali

Sierra Leone

Nigeria

Djibouti

Cape Verde

Sudan

South Sudan

Egypt

Mauritania

Gambia

Liberia

Senegal

Guinea-Bissau

Central African Republic

Democratic Republic of the Congo

Uganda

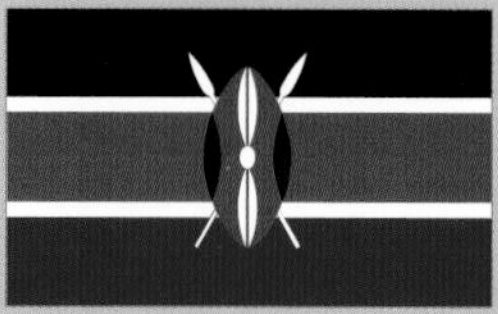

Kenya

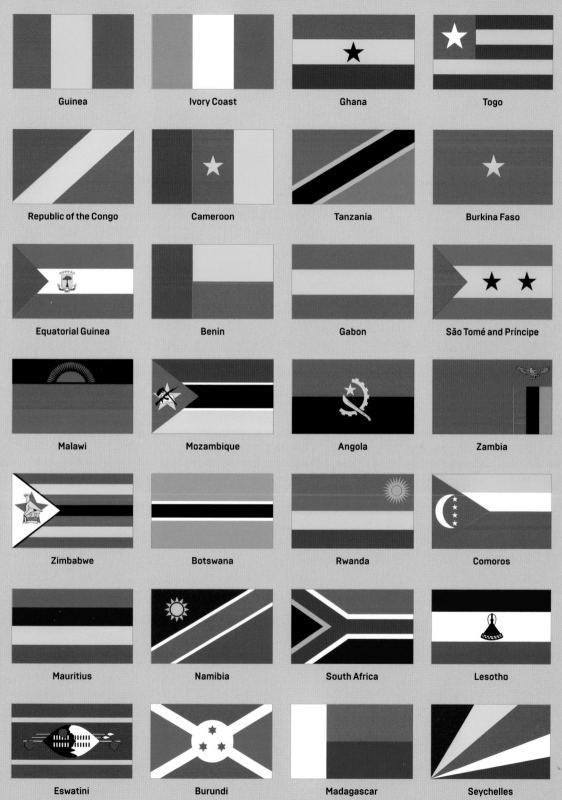

Guinea

Ivory Coast

Ghana

Togo

Republic of the Congo

Cameroon

Tanzania

Burkina Faso

Equatorial Guinea

Benin

Gabon

São Tomé and Príncipe

Malawi

Mozambique

Angola

Zambia

Zimbabwe

Botswana

Rwanda

Comoros

Mauritius

Namibia

South Africa

Lesotho

Eswatini

Burundi

Madagascar

Seychelles

NORTH, CENTRAL AND SOUTH AMERICA

Canada

Mexico

United States of America

Belize

Honduras

El Salvador

Costa Rica

Panama

Cuba

Jamaica

Bahamas

Haiti

Dominican Republic

Antigua and Barbuda

Puerto Rico

Dominica

Saint Lucia

Barbados

Grenada

Saint Vincent and the Grenadines

Venezuela

Saint Kitts and Nevis

Guyana

Suriname

Trinidad and Tobago

Colombia

Ecuador

Brazil

Peru

Bolivia

Chile

Argentina

Uruguay

Paraguay

Guatemala

Nicaragua

Index

Elisabeth Dumont-Le Cornec's Acknowledgments

Béatrice, thanks to whom this new editorial adventure began; Philippe and Nicolas, from Olo Éditions, who placed their full trust in me; Sara, who has shown immense patience, diplomacy and talent; Élise, who brilliantly worked the layout to integrate all the flags; Nadja, Laurence and Maia, who enriched the galleries; my family and friends, who provided me with ideas and support.

Editor's Acknowledgments

The site flagstories.co, which inspired some parts of this book.

IMAGE CREDITS

© Alamy: p. 11: mccool/Alamy Stock Photo; p. 27: Historical image collection by Bildagentur-online/Alamy Stock Photo; p. 109: World History Archive/Alamy Stock Photo; p. 137: PRISMA ARCHIVO/Alamy Stock Photo; pp. 156-157: Colin Harris/eraimages/Alamy Stock Photo.

© Getty Images: p. 17: DeAgostini/Getty Images; p. 51: Fine Art Images/Heritage Images via Getty Images; p. 67: Keystone/Getty Images; p. 99: Leemage/Corbis via Getty Images; p. 93: Chris Jackson/Getty Images; pp. 94-95: Staff/Mirrorpix via Getty Images; p. 147: George Rinhart/Corbis via Getty Images; p. 153: Keystone-France/Gamma-Keystone via Getty Images; p. 163: José Luis Quintana/LatinContent via Getty Images; p. 168: Michele Amoruso/Pacific Press/LightRocket via Getty Images; pp. 172-173: Scott Peterson/Liaison/Getty Images; p. 178: Mansell/Mansell/The LIFE Picture Collection via Getty Images; p. 181: Vladimir Rys/Bongarts/Getty Images; p. 187: Culture Club/Getty Images; p. 188: Matthew Chattle/Barcroft Media via Getty Images.

© Library of Congress: pp. 18-19: Harris & Ewing, photographer/Library of Congress; p. 123: National Photo Company Collection/Library of Congress; pp. 132-133: Library of Congress; p. 151: H.A. Thomas & Wylie/Weisgerber, Charles H., artist/Library of Congress.

© Shutterstock: pp. 124-125: Wangkun Jia/Shutterstock.com; p. 170: Zvonimir Atletic/Shutterstock.com; p. 171: Bernsten/Shutterstock.com; p. 183: Ryan Fowler Photography/Shutterstock.com; pp. 238-239: Iurii Osadchi/Shutterstock.com.

© DR: p. 71; p. 75; p. 113.